bright and bold

nursery crafts

*for
olive + nick
xox*

acknowledgements
I would like to thank the following people for their help
Simon Blackall and Diane Wallis for photography, poems and dinners
Nick Godlee for clever ideas and tricky sewing tips
Tony Sheringbone for computer consultation and tenuous titles
Cathy Campbell for making sense of the mess
and all the lovely babies who modelled
Ellen Moran
Nicholas Robson
Olive Godlee
Ella Butler
Audrey Abbott (and her mum Susie)

Copyright © Sophie Blackall 1998
All rights reserved. No part of this publication may be reproduced, stored
in a retrieval system or transmitted in any form or by any means electronic,
mechanical, photocopying or otherwise without first obtaining written permission
from the copyright owner.

This edition published in 1998 by The Watermark Press,
Sydney, Australia
Designer: Sophie Blackall
ISBN 0 949284 37 8
Printed by L. Rex Printing, China
10 9 8 7 6 5 4 3 2 1
National Library of Australia
Cataloguing-in-Publication Data:

    Blackall, Sophie.
        Bright & bold nursery crafts
        ISBN 0 949284 37 8
        1. Toy making. 2. Children's furniture. 3. House
        furnishings. 4. Handycraft. I. Title
        745.5

bright and bold
nursery crafts

by Sophie Blackall

The Watermark Press

contents

introduction 6

playtime

giraffe 12
elephant 14
monkey 16
cloth book 19
noah's ark 24
play mat 33
string of toys 37

dinnertime

bright bibs 42
nursing cushion 47
feeding chair holdall 49

 # bathtime

bath toy bag 55
bunny towel 57
change mat 60
clothes tidy 65

bedtime

jigsaw cushions 70
alphabet bumper 75
mobile 78
insect quilt 83
stencils 91

introduction

My mother made us some wonderful things when we were babies. I remember a much loved quilt with flowers and ducks and toadstools, and a princess and the pea wall hanging with appliquéd mattresses all stacked up and a green bead underneath them. The fabrics she used are as evocative as smells and take me straight back to my childhood. When I found out I was having a baby, I was very pleased to have an excuse to make lovely baby things. I set out to find a book to inspire me, and was struck by the lack of anything remotely contemporary. It was all pastel teddy bears and lace edged bunny suits with 'baby' in cross-stitch...very pretty, but I think most people can distinguish the baby without it being labelled!

    A couple of years later, I have finally finished this book; a selection of fun, useful and decorative things to make, all of which have been tried and tested by babies and parents. Most of the projects are easy and inexpensive to make, and use bright, bold, contemporary colours and fabrics. Some are designed to be made quickly and easily, thrashed to death and thrown away when your baby grows out of them. Others have the potential to be passed from child to child and be the stuff of fond memories. Either way I hope you and your babies enjoy them.

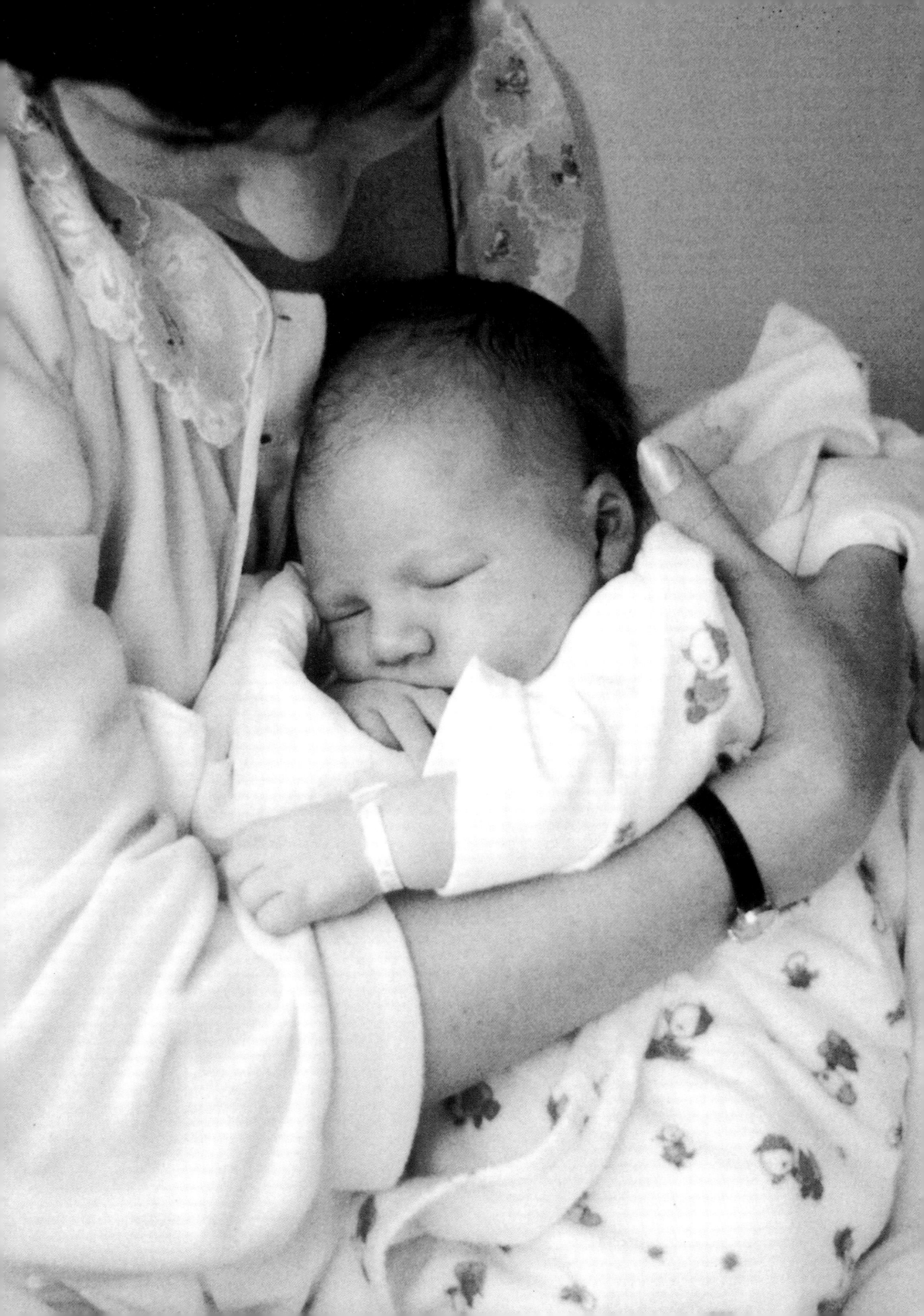

playtime

Now it's time for us to play
And learn new words throughout the day.
We crawl, then walk, to much acclaim
And, after smiles repeat the same.

But then we chance upon the swings
And upward soar on secret wings,
Then swoop back down in icy fear
To waiting faces warm and dear.

Our joy in living should be shared
With other children so prepared
That as we walk, then run, then climb
Our friends are with us all the time.

How nice to be alive.

elephant giraffe monkey

These friendly animal toys have jointed legs and tails and bright glass eyes. When squeezed they have a surprising squeaky voice! I gave them to my daughter when she turned one and was more or less past the everything straight into the mouth stage… before then they smiled down at her from the safety of the nursery shelf. The animals were made by hand using blanket stitch, but they could easily be machine sewn.

general directions

These toys are actually very easy to make. Each body is made from two pieces of felt with a gusset (just a long strip) between them. The details are put on the flat pieces first, then they are sewn together using blanket (or loop) stitch and stuffed 'as you go' with scraps of wadding.

The legs are two pieces sewn together and stuffed in the same way. Legs and tails are attached to the body with buttons, which allow them to move backwards and forwards.

To make these toys on the sewing machine, add 1cm (⅜in) seam allowance to each pattern. Sew pieces together in the same order as if assembled by hand, clipping into corners and curves as necessary. Leave a gap to turn the piece through, then stuff, using a crochet hook or something similar to push the wadding into narrow legs etc.

TIPS ✿ When making anything for babies that has small parts, you need to take particular care to ensure the parts cannot be removed and consequently swallowed (or inserted into ears or noses).

✿ Only use animal eyes with a backing which, once assembled, cannot be removed.

✿ Test that buttons are secure by pulling on them with full strength.

✿ Use good quality, strong thread.

blanket or loop stitch

giraffe

materials
- 30cm (12in) yellow felt
- One square brown felt
- Scrap of pink felt
- Two small 5 mm (¼in) toy animal eyes with safety backings
- Polyester stuffing or wadding
- Yellow, brown and black thread
- Squeaker (available from craft supply stores)
- Five 10mm (⅜in) white buttons

TIP ✿ Felt can be bought in squares (approximately 30cm (12in) in size), or by the metre. There is usually a wider range of colours in the squares.

preparation

Trace head and neck, body, leg, eyelid and ear pattern pieces onto yellow felt. Trace foot bases, feet, horns and patches onto brown felt. Trace pink inner ears onto pink felt. Mark positions of eyes and buttons. Cut out pieces according to directions on patterns.

Measure and cut a gusset 2cm (¾in) wide by 38 cm (15in) long from yellow felt.

Attach the eye in position on each head.

Don't forget to make one giraffe face each way (in mirror reverse).

Sew a row of blanket stitch in black thread along the lower edge of each eyelid to form eyelashes. Lay the eyelid over the top third of each eye and sew the eyelid down along the top curve in yellow thread.

Embroider the mouth and nostrils on each head piece in black thread. Sew the brown patches in place on each head and neck piece, each body side and on the top of each leg.

You don't need to put any patches where the neck covers the body.

TIP ✿ I actually sewed the patches on by machine in straight stitch. It was much quicker and didn't spoil the hand sewn look. Use brown thread and clip all loose threads to finish.

assembly

Sew the ears together in pairs and stitch a pink inner ear in place on top.

Place two giraffe necks with wrong sides together. Insert the still folded inner neck piece so that it lines up with the lower necks of the other two pieces. Beginning at the top of the fold, sew one half of the inner neck to one outer neck edge. When you reach the fold again, continue down the other side, sewing the other half of the inner neck to the other outer neck edge. Pause at this point. If you peel the two heads apart, you should have two pockets at the base of the neck. Insert some wadding evenly into these pockets so that they are padded but not fat.

Continue to sew the head pieces together, pausing to sew the brown horns and inner horns in the same manner as the base of the neck. Insert stuffing as you go. Complete the last side and finish with a secure knot. Sew the ears onto each side of the head.

Sew the brown feet to the bottom outer side of each leg. Starting at the foot, sew each pair of legs together, working stuffing in as before. When you arrive at the other lower edge, sew the foot base into place. Starting at the notch mark, sew one long edge of the gusset around the edge of one body piece, leaving the first 3mm (⅛in) of the gusset free. Attach the second body piece to the other long edge of the gusset, making sure the bodies line up exactly.

Insert the squeaker with the stuffing. Sew the two ends of the gusset together where they meet at the notch. Sew the two tail pieces together, inserting a scrap of stuffing, and leaving the end open.

Make a tassel tail end by wrapping black thread around two fingers several times. Tie one end of the bundle through the loop and bind securely. Clip through other ends and insert tassel top into tail end. Stitch firmly in place.

With long pins, attach the legs to the body using the marks as guides. Sew buttons onto back legs, through the body out to the other side. Use a strong double thread and test that buttons are sewn securely. Repeat for the front legs. Attach the neck to the body in the same way, and the tail.

The giraffe's mane is made from a long row of knotted threads, tied and clipped short.

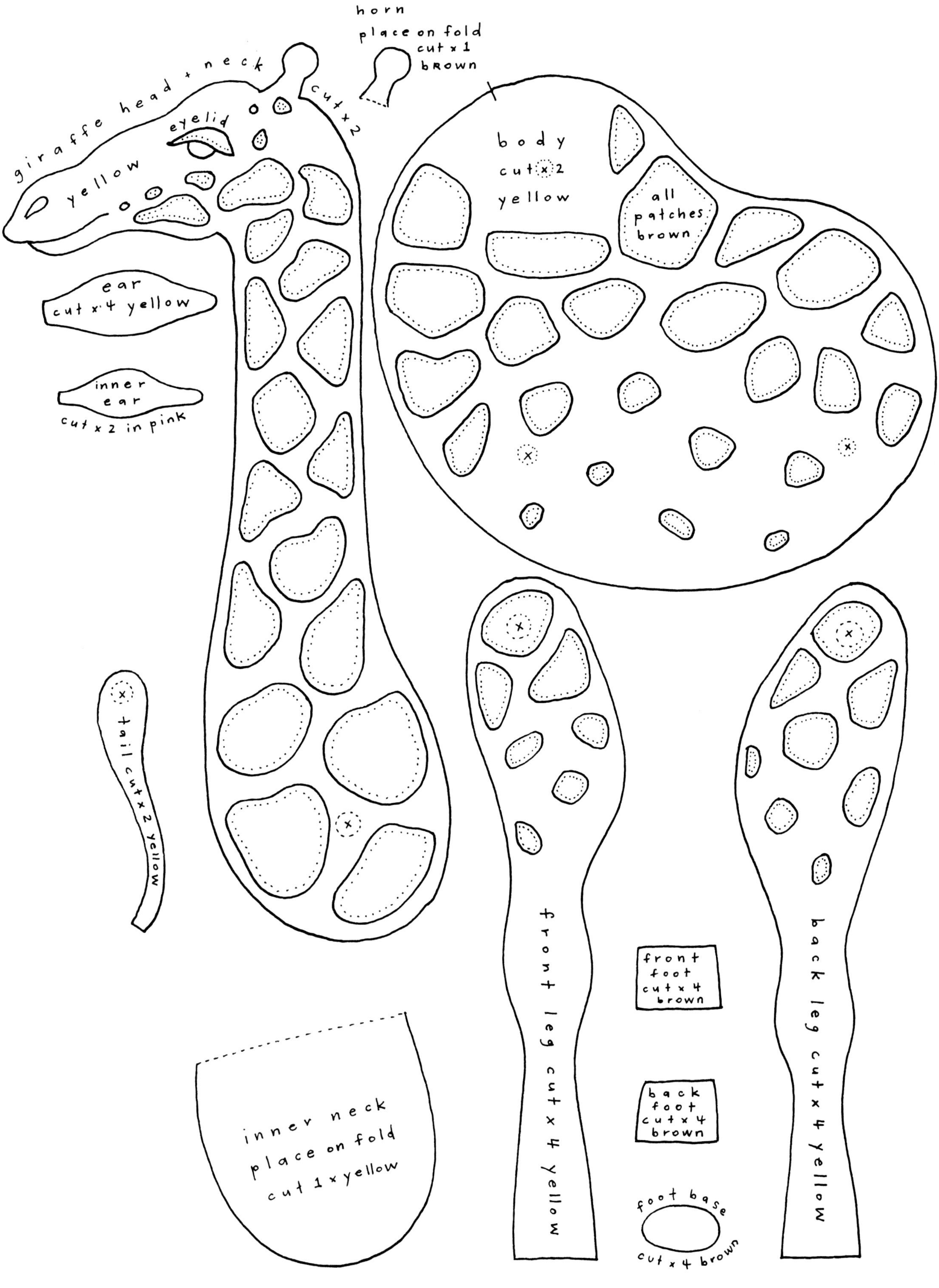

horn
place on fold
cut x 1
brown
giraffe head + neck
cut x 2
eyelid
yellow
body
cut x 2
yellow
all patches brown
ear
cut x 4 yellow
inner ear
cut x 2 in pink
tail cut x 2 yellow
front leg cut x 4 yellow
back leg cut x 4 yellow
front foot
cut x 4
brown
back foot
cut x 4
brown
inner neck
place on fold
cut 1 x yellow
foot base
cut x 4 brown

elephant

materials
- 30cm (12in) dark grey felt
- One square light grey felt
- Scrap of pink felt
- Scrap of white felt
- Two small 5mm (¼in) toy eyes with safety backings
- Polyester stuffing or wadding
- Grey, white and black thread
- Squeaker (available from craft supply stores)
- Five 10mm (⅜in) white buttons

preparation
Trace head, body, leg, foot base, tail and ear pattern pieces onto dark grey felt. Trace inside ear onto light grey felt. Trace inside trunk piece onto pink felt.

Mark positions of eyes, cheeks, ears and buttons and cut out pieces according to pattern directions Measure and cut a gusset 3cm (1¼in) wide by 64cm (26in) long from dark grey felt. Attach the eye in position on each head and stitch eyelid line in black thread. Don't forget to make one elephant face each way (mirror reverse).

Stitch along the cheek line, then carefully cut below the stitches with a craft knife between the notches marked on the pattern. Repeat for the other piece. Don't forget to flip it so that it is in mirror reverse.

Sew tusk pairs together in white thread, inserting a tiny piece of stuffing. Place the tusks curving upwards into the cheek slits. Sew along the cheek line and backstitch to secure tusks in position.

assembly
Using blanket stitch, sew ears together in pairs of one light grey and one dark grey, stuffing with a scrap of wadding. Sew the ears in place on each side of head.

Beginning at the end of the trunk, sew one long edge of the gusset strip to one body piece. Attach the second body piece to the other side of the gusset, stopping at the top of the head to stuff body and insert squeaker. Continue to sew down the trunk, working stuffing in as you go.

Fit pink felt shape into trunk end and stitch in place. Position toenails on the base of legs and sew.

Sew pairs of long legs together, from base to base. Stuff, then fit circular foot base into place and stitch. Repeat for short legs.

Sew the two tail pieces together, inserting a scrap of stuffing and leaving the end open.

Make a tassel tail end by wrapping black thread around two fingers several times. Tie one end of the bundle through the loop and bind securely.

Clip through other ends and insert tassel top into tail end. Stitch firmly in place.

With long pins, attach the legs to the body using the marks as guides.

Sew the first button onto one of the back legs, pushing the needle through the body out to the other side. Pierce through the second leg and button on that side to secure them in the same way.

Repeat this process a couple of times. Use a strong double thread and test that buttons are sewn securely.

NOTE ✿ Take care not to compress the body when pulling the thread taut.

Repeat for the front legs. Attach the tail to the body in the same way.

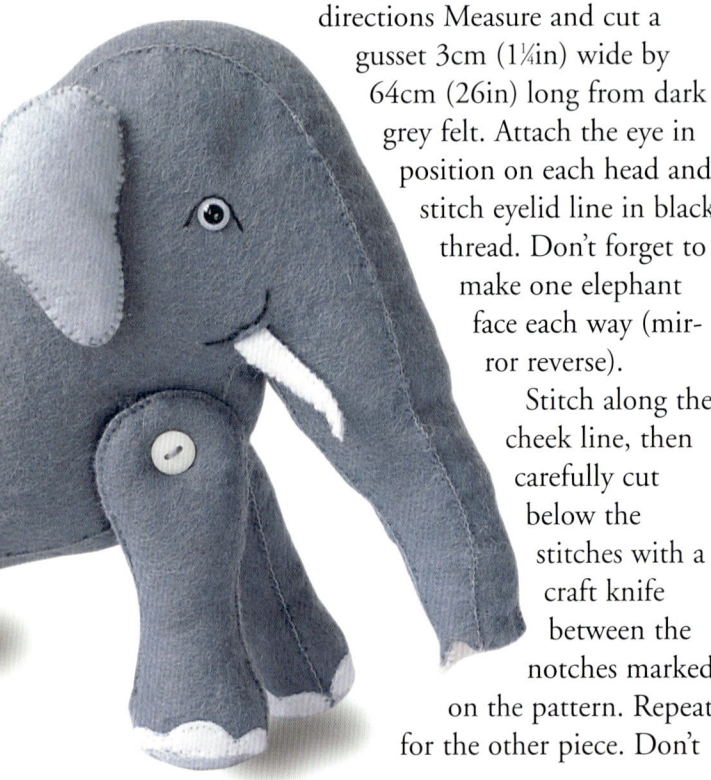

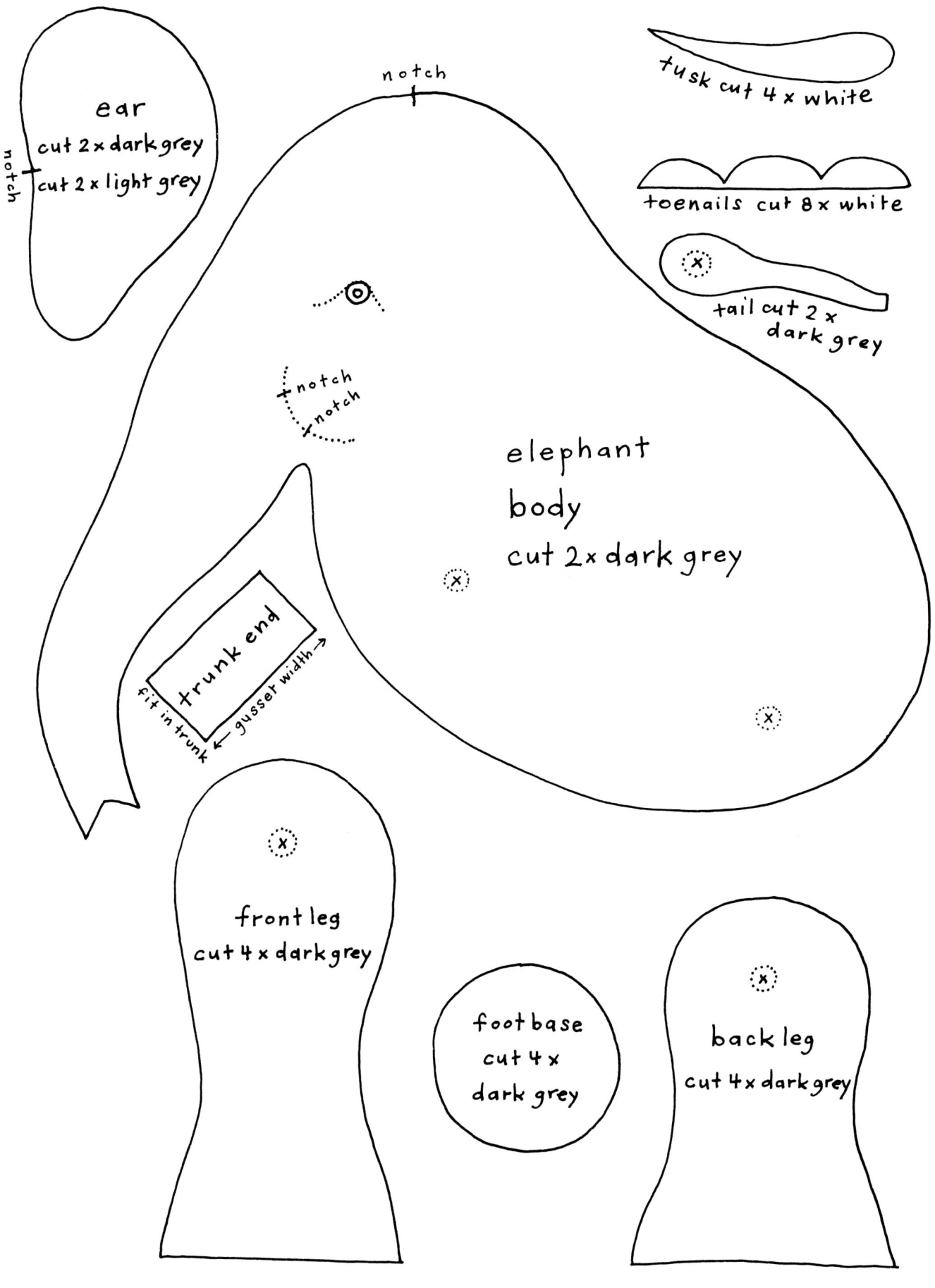

monkey

materials
- 30cm (12in) red felt
- One square pink felt
- Two small 5mm (¼in) toy eyes with safety backings
- Polyester stuffing or wadding
- Red, pink and black thread
- Squeaker(available from craft supply stores)
- Five 10mm (⅜in) white buttons
- One pipe cleaner

preparation
Trace body, leg, tail and ear patterns onto red felt. Onto pink felt, trace feet, face and inner ears.

Mark positions of eyes and buttons.

Cut out pieces according to directions on patterns.

Measure and cut a gusset 1cm (⅜in) wide by 37cm (14½in) long from red felt.

Cut a small pink gusset 1cm (⅜in) wide by 5cm (2in) long, which is sewn overlapping the red gusset to give the face width.

Sew each face in position on each red body, making sure to make one monkey facing each way.

Attach the eye in position on each head and embroider the mouth and nostrils in black thread.

assembly
Sew the ears together in pairs of outer red and inner pink. Attach the ears onto each side of the head.

Sew the pink feet to the bottom outer side of each leg. Starting at the lower edge of the foot, sew each pair of legs together, left and right, front and back, working stuffing in as before.

Beginning where the tail will join the body, sew one long edge of the gusset around the edge of one body piece, leaving the first 3mm (⅛in) of the gusset free.

When you reach the lower edge of the face (chin), match the pink gusset piece to the lower cheek line, catching it in as you sew the main gusset.

Attach the second body piece to the other long edge of the gusset, making sure the bodies line up exactly.

Insert the squeaker with the stuffing.

Sew the two ends of the gusset together where they meet. This join will be disguised by the tail.

Start to sew the tail pieces together, sandwiching a spiralled pipe cleaner wrapped in stuffing between the two layers of felt.

Continue to sew up the tail, enclosing the wire. This keeps the tail in shape. When you reach the base of the tail, insert folded inner piece and sew in place.

With long pins, attach the legs to the body using the button marks as guides. Sew buttons onto back legs, through the body out to the other side, through those legs and buttons and back again.

Use a strong double thread and test that buttons are sewn securely. Repeat for the front legs. Attach the tail to the body in the same way, adjusting the curve of the pipe cleaner.

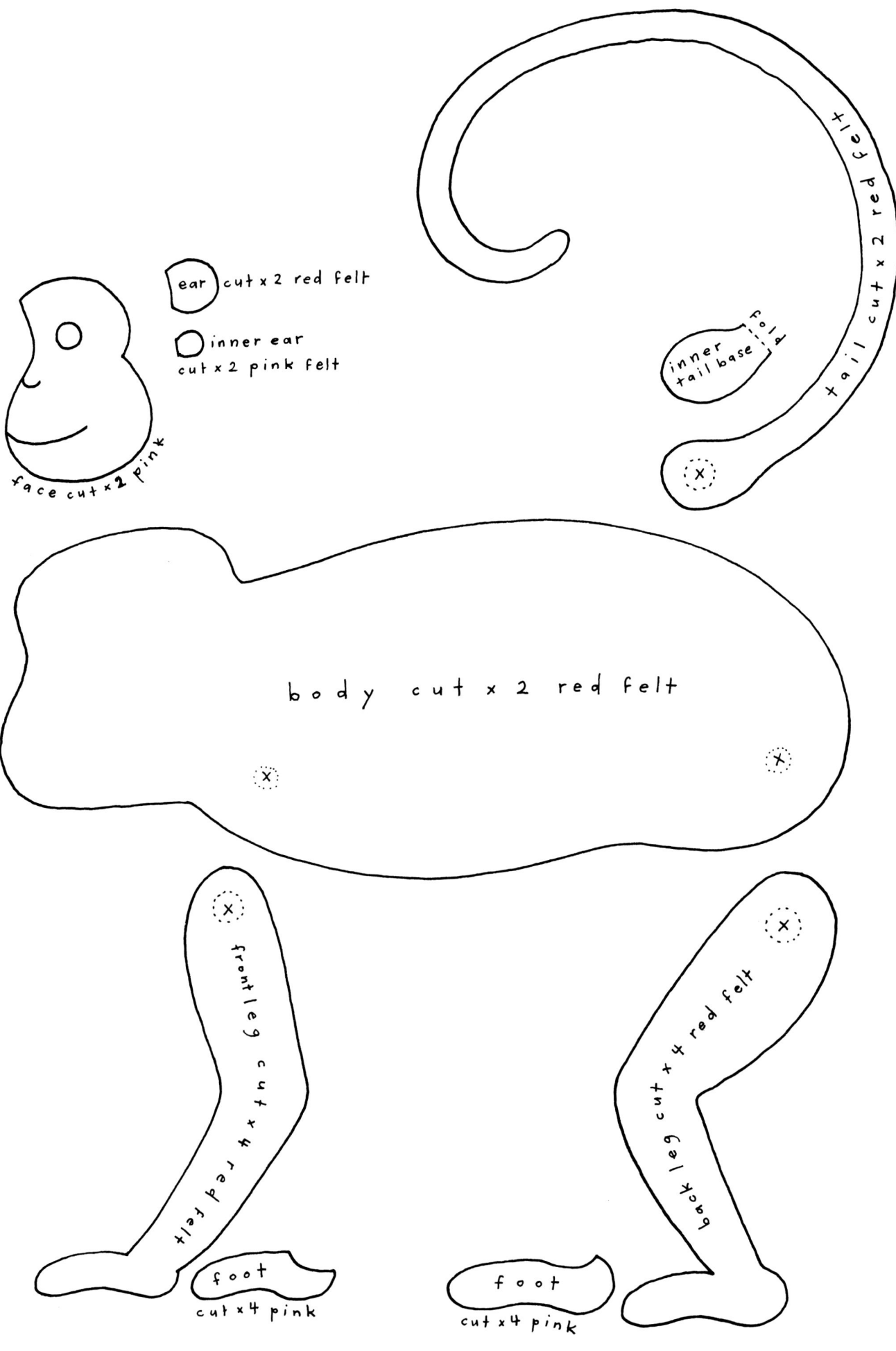

clothbook

Fabric books are bright, colourful and tactile, and are a wonderful introduction to real books. This one has a clothing theme and uses materials like satin, felt, velvet, suede and linen. You could choose any theme that inspires you; have a look in the pattern pages for other designs. Consider a series of fruit and vegetables, or toys or animals or a personalised book of your family. My baby used to go to bed with her cloth book and fall asleep with the pages covering her face.

materials

- 20cm (8in) each of red, white, blue and yellow cotton, (or colours of your choice)
- 20cm (8in) of 5mm (¼in) thick fusible wadding
- 20cm (8in) fusible web
- Assorted fabric scraps (go through your scrap bag to find interesting fabrics, or have a look in the remnant bin in your local haberdashery)
- Buttons, beads, scraps of lace or trims
- Coloured sewing thread
- Fading marker pen

preparation

Trace all pattern elements (e.g. overalls plus pockets and cuffs) onto fusible web paper. Cut roughly around each shape. Decide on fabrics to be used for each picture.

some fabric suggestions

SWIMMING COSTUME ✿ satin, lycra, polished cotton
SHOE ✿ leather, vinyl, suede
UNDERPANTS ✿ silk, satin, cotton, lace
DRESS ✿ cotton prints (floral, polka dot)
OVERALLS ✿ cotton checks or stripes
COAT ✿ wool, velvet or felt, with lining in cotton
SOCK ✿ wool, knit fabric, felt
CAP ✿ coloured cotton drill

Using a hot steam iron, fuse web pattern shapes (with paper attached) to appropriate pieces of fabric.

Cut out neatly, and assemble individual clothing pictures, still leaving backing paper intact. With the coat for example, put the lining piece down first, then arrange the front coat flaps and finally the contrasting cuffs. Remove the backing paper from the cuffs first, and fuse in place on the coat sleeves, pressing down with a hot steam iron for several seconds.

TIP ✿ When ironing, use a scrap of cotton fabric as a pressing cloth to protect your work.

Remove paper from coat flaps and fuse to coat lining (which still has its backing paper). Repeat to this stage for all pictures.

With the fading marker pen, trace two 14cm (5½in) squares side by side on each of the four pieces of coloured cotton fabric.

Cut around rectangles, leaving at least 2cm (¾in) seam allowance.

assembly

Place a picture on each square page in whichever order you like. One by one remove backing paper and fuse in place. When cool, test that all pieces are firmly bonded to the page by trying to peel back layers. If in doubt, press each picture again.
Next, top stitch around each piece of the picture in the appropriate coloured thread which will make appliqué strong enough to survive machine washing.

TIP ✿ **To reduce the number of times you have to rethread your machine, sew everything of one colour first, then rethread with the second colour and so on, rather than working picture by picture.**

Cut four 14cm (5½in) squares of fusible wadding. Arrange two squares side by side on the wrong side of one fabric rectangle, leaving a tiny gap along what will be the spine of the book. Repeat with the other two wadding squares on a second rectangle. Organize the four rectangles in pairs of one wadding and one non-wadding, with right sides together, making sure the pictures are all the right way up. Sew around each, leaving an opening of about 5cm (2in).

TIP ✿ **The end result will be neater if you leave a seam opening in the middle of an edge rather then at a corner.**

Turn through to right side and press. Top stitch each rectangle with the appropriate coloured thread for needle and bobbin, at the same time closing the gap. Place one rectangle on top of the other and line edges up neatly. Stitch down the centre line to divide the pages, sewing through all layers. Repeat line of stitching for strength; this forms the spine of the book.

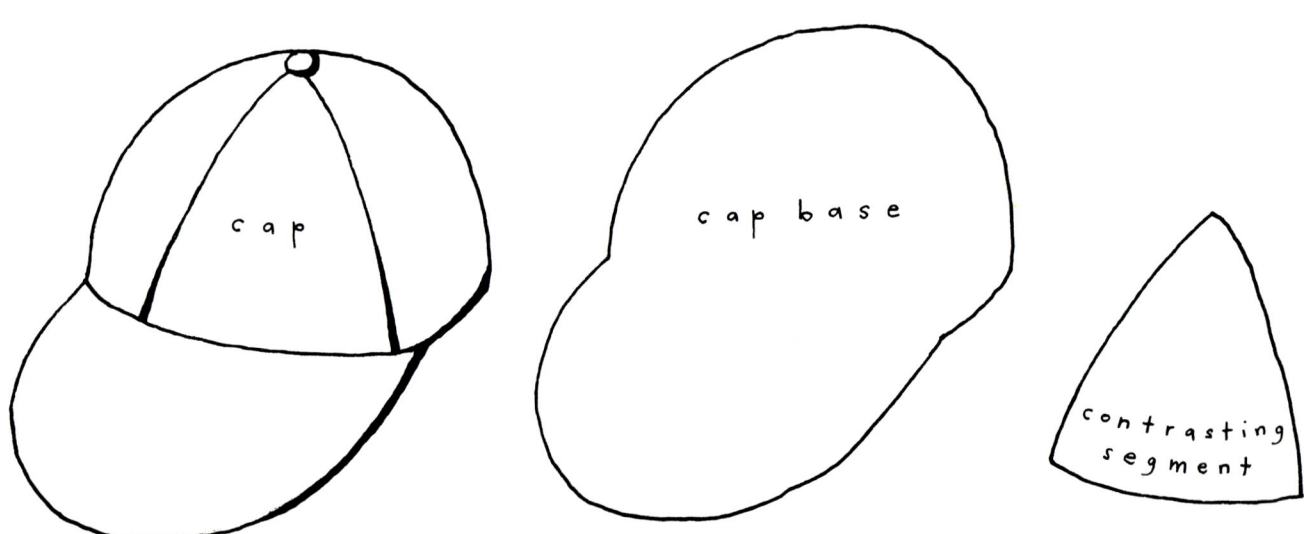

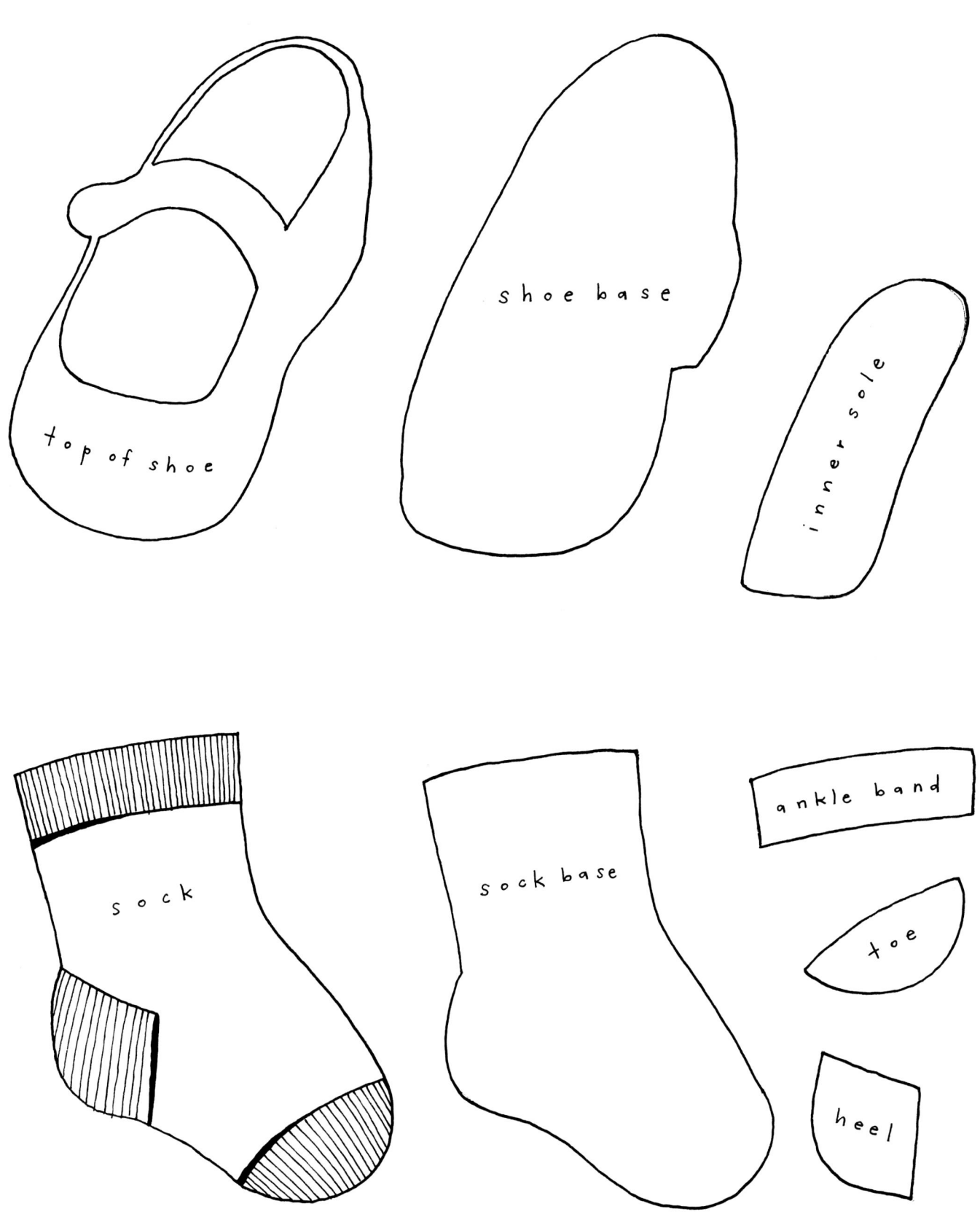

noah's ark

This imaginative Noah's Ark wall hanging will fascinate a little baby with its bright colours and shapes, amuse a toddler who can take the animals out and put them back in, and entertain the small child who can name them and play at putting them to bed. Noah's Ark is appliquéd in colourful cotton drill with a stormy sea and rain clouds. Mr and Mrs Noah and the animals are stencilled with fabric paints and made into little stuffed toys. Their silhouettes are also stencilled in their places, to make a game of putting them away. Pockets sewn onto the ark form beds, each with top sheet and blanket, for the animals when they get tired.

materials

for Mr and Mrs noah and the animals
- 40cm (½yd) white cotton drill
- 40cm (½yd) black cotton drill
- Polyester stuffing
- 5 sheets approx. 21cm x 30cm (8½in x 12in) acetate or stencil film (clear plastic film from craft stores)
- Fabric paint in red, blue, yellow, black and white
- Fading marker pen
- Waterproof marker pen (fine line)
- Craft knife
- Stencil brush or sponges
- Paper towels
- Old newspaper
- Pressing cloth (scrap of clean cotton fabric)
- White thread

for the wall hanging
- 30cm (12in) white cotton drill (for the beds)
- 20cm (8in) white cotton (sheets)
- 30cm (12in) grey striped wool fabric (blankets)
- 50cm (20in) red cotton drill (ark)
- 140cm (1½yd) blue cotton drill (background)
- 20cm (8in) green cotton drill (sea)
- 20cm (8in) light green cotton drill (sea)
- 20cm (8in) grey cotton drill (clouds)
- 20cm (8in) beige cotton drill (Noah's room)
- 10cm (4in) brown cotton drill (roof)
- 10cm (4in) black cotton drill (umbrella)
- Two 65cm (26in) lengths wooden dowel
- Sewing thread in white, black, red, grey, blue, green, light green, beige and brown
- 60cm (24in) fusible web (at least 65cm [26in] wide)
- 60cm (24in) iron-on interfacing
- Coloured carbon paper
- Tracing wheel

preparation

animals
With the waterproof pen, trace stencil patterns onto stencil film or acetate, making sure there is at least 2cm (¾in) room around each pattern. If an animal has more than one colour, you will need to trace it more than once. Mr and Mrs Noah need to be traced four times.

Cut the acetate sheets so that each pattern is on a separate piece (still with 2cm all around).

Using a craft knife, carefully cut out the windows of each pattern for each colour. With the giraffe, for example, you will need to cut the basic body shape out of one piece to be stencilled in yellow, then the spots out of the second piece to be stencilled in black over the top.

Prepare the white cotton drill to be stencilled. You may find it easier to cut the fabric into pieces (the size of the largest animal pattern with at least 3cm all around).

TIP ✿ It is a good idea to prewash and iron all fabric before use, to eliminate possible shrinkage or colour bleeding.

✿ For detailed stencilling directions, see page 91.

Begin stencilling the animal designs onto the fabric. Choose one base colour to start and complete all areas of all patterns before moving to the next colour. Only the lions and Mr and Mrs Noah have a male and female, the other animals use the same design in mirror image. Make sure you clean all excess paint from the stencil with a cloth or paper towel before placing face down on the fabric.

When base colours are completely dry, apply second colours, then third and so on.

some suggestions for paint order

YELLOW ✿ lioness (head and body), lion (body only), giraffe left and right.
RED ✿ Noah's shirt, Mrs Noah's skirt, monkey left and right.
GREY (WHITE + BLACK) ✿ elephant left and right, rabbit left and right.
DARK GREEN (BLUE + YELLOW) ✿ tortoise body left and right.

(By this time the yellow should be dry)

ORANGE (RED + YELLOW) ✿ kangaroo left and right, lion's mane (overlapping body).
PINK (WHITE + RED) ✿ flamingo body left and right, rabbits' ears, monkeys' faces and ears, Noah and Mrs Noah's faces.
LIGHT GREEN (YELLOW + BLUE) ✿ tortoiseshell left and right.
BLUE ✿ Noah's trousers, Mrs Noah's blouse.
BLACK ✿ giraffes' spots left and right, flamingos' legs and beaks left and right, Noah and Mrs Noah's hair and feet.
WHITE ✿ elephant toes and tusks left and right.

When everything is dry, fix fabric paint according to manufacturer's directions, usually this is pressing with a steam iron for several seconds. Use a pressing cloth (any clean piece of cotton fabric) to protect your work and the iron.

Draw outlines and faces with a waterproof marker.

Cut out animals 1cm (⅜in) from edge of design and place face down on black drill. Cut out, and with right sides still together, sew 5mm (¼in) in from edge (leaving a 3cm (1¼in) gap in a discreet place for turning through). Reinforce corners and clip into curves. Turn through to right side using a crochet hook or chopstick to ease out long narrow legs and tails.

Press again and stuff using your crochet hook to work the stuffing into all corners.

Sew up the opening by hand with a neat stitch.

Noah's ark

Mark out bed rectangles on white drill. (See ark pattern on page 31.) Press fusible web to wrong side, leaving paper intact, and cut out rectangles.

TIP ✿ **You can place rectangles side by side, which will save fabric and fusible web and make cutting out easier.**

Using black fabric paint, stencil silhouettes of animals and Noahs in mirrored (or male/female) pairs on the appropriate bed rectangles.

NOTE ✿ **Giraffe necks extend above the ark, so will be stencilled later onto blue sky.**

Enlarge ark pattern by 400% and trace onto red drill. Apply iron-on interfacing to wrong side.

Trace the pattern for Noah's room onto beige drill. Apply iron-on interfacing to wrong side and cut out. Repeat for the roof on brown drill.

Using coloured carbon paper and a tracing wheel, mark positions of beds onto ark shape.

Remove backing paper and with a steam iron and pressing cloth fuse the white animals' beds in place on the red ark and the Noahs' bed in place on the beige rectangle. This will also fix the fabric paint.

To make top sheets, cut white cotton into 6cm (2½in) strips. Fold in half and press as you would when making bias binding.

Trace blanket patterns (coloured areas on ark pattern) onto grey wool fabric and cut out, remembering to leave 1cm (⅜in) all around to be turned under.

Align the cut edges of the sheet strips along the top edge of each blanket (cut the strips to the right length). Sew 1cm (⅜in) in from top.

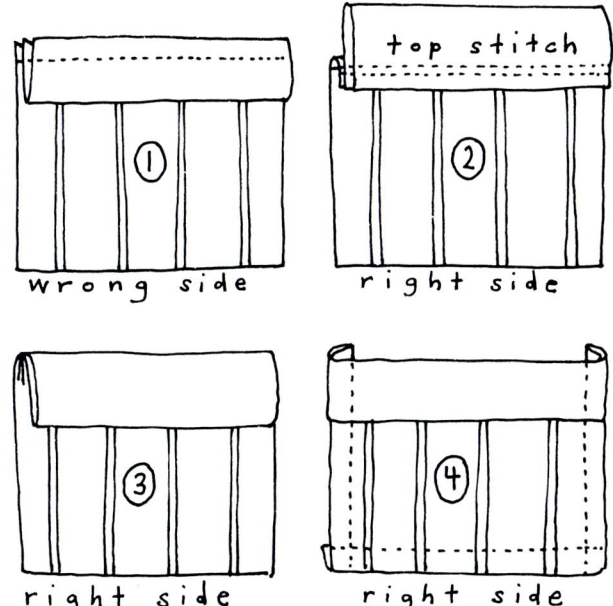

Repeat for each blanket. Fold and press as shown in the diagram above. Sew down cut edges. Fold sides and bottom edges under and press.

Position blankets on beds, pin and top stitch down.

assembly

Cut out blue background fabric into two rectangles 70cm x 80cm (27½in x 31½in).

Fold the roof edges under and press. Repeat for Noah's room. Position the roof over Noah's room and place both on the blue background fabric. Cut out the ark shape and position over the bottom edge of Noah's room. Pin all in place.

Top stitch room and roof in brown thread. Sew around ark in straight stitch first, (using red thread), then in close zig-zag (appliqué stitch) around the top and sides only.

Complete the stencilled giraffe silhouettes, extending their necks and heads onto the blue. Fix paint.

Cut strips 10cm x 70cm (4in x 27½in) of dark green, light green and grey drill for the sea and clouds. apply fusible web to the wrong side of each of these strips, leaving backing paper intact.

Cut scallop template (four semi-circles side by side) out of cardboard. Place straight edge of template along the top edges of light and dark green drill (on the paper side) and trace and repeat to make waves.

Invert template and repeat along the top edge of the grey strip to form clouds. With sharp scissors, cut along wave and cloud scalloped edges.

Remove backing paper and position on wall hanging; clouds up the top and waves at the bottom (overlapping the lower edge of the ark). Fuse in place. Zig-zag (appliqué stitch) along cloud and wave edges in the appropriate thread.

For the umbrella, apply fusible web to the wrong side of a piece of black drill. Trace umbrella pattern onto paper side and cut out. Remove paper, place above giraffes' heads and fuse in position.

In black thread, zig-zag around umbrella and down between the giraffes to form the umbrella handle.

Top stitch the white lines on umbrella and roof.

TIP ✿ Use your machine foot as a guide to space the lines on the roof evenly.

With right sides together, align the two blue rectangles. Pin together and sew around, leaving a gap in the middle of the bottom edge. Turn through to right side and press seams. Close gap by hand.

Stencil raindrops in the sky in white fabric paint. Make them bounce off the umbrella by changing their direction. Press to fix paint.

Attach dowel rods to the back of the wall hanging at top and bottom, using a needle and strong thread. Bring needle through the back of fabric, around the rod and back through the fabric. Repeat the length of each rod and knot thread securely to finish.

The fun part is arranging Mr and Mrs Noah and the animals in their beds, by which time you will probably want to get into bed too.

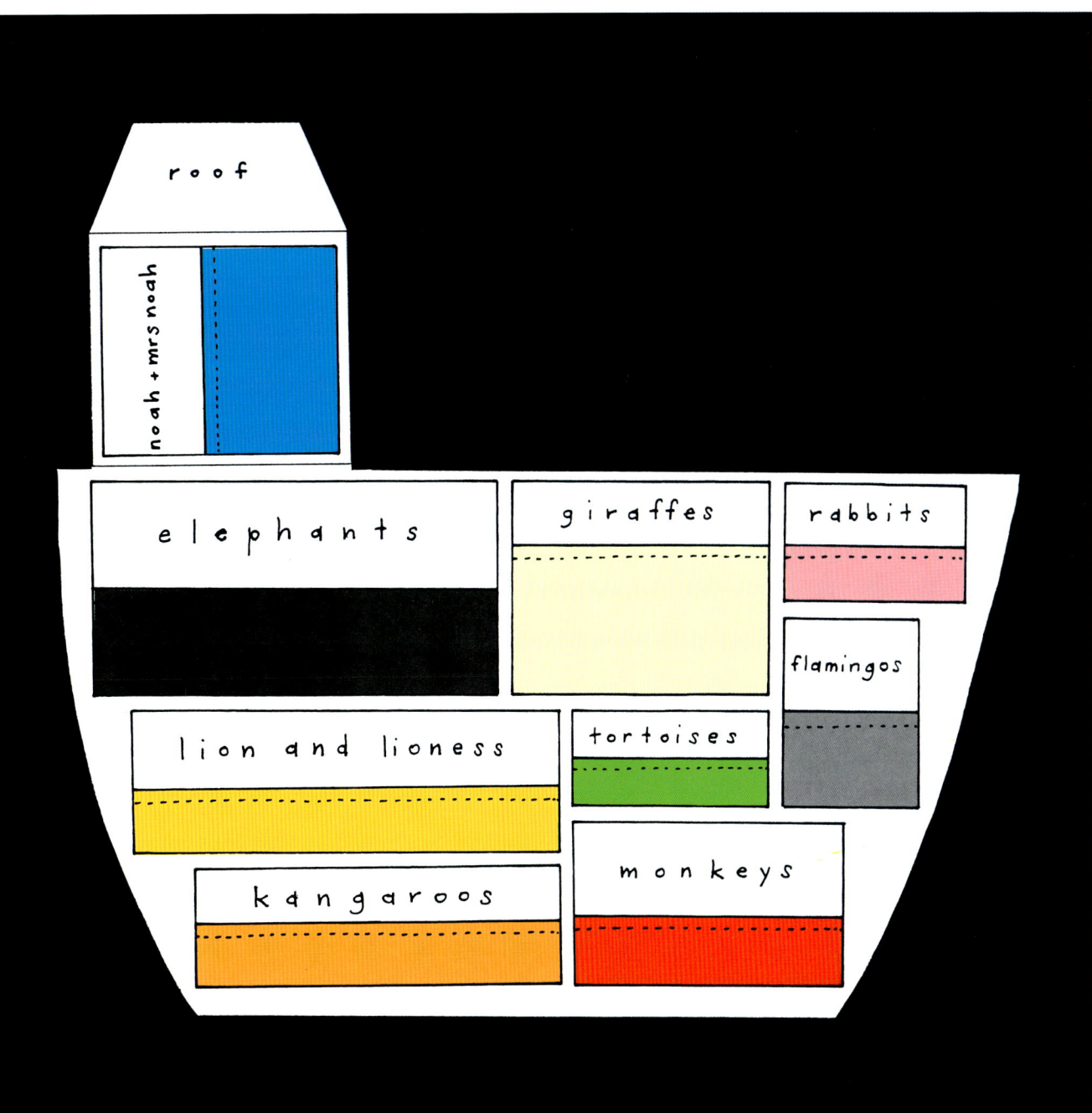

play mat

This is a great idea. The circular playmat converts into a convenient toy bag, so when you need to make a quick getaway from the park you simply pull up the drawstrings and everything is scooped up neatly. I made this with a bright target design of coloured concentric circles, but you could paint flowers, a giant face, or a road map for babies who like to play with cars. You could vary the design on each side as the playmat/bag is reversible, and if your baby is up to painting and you're feeling brave, you could get her to help. You can't go wrong with hand prints.

materials

- 120cm (1⅓yd) heavy canvas (from art supply stores, hardware stores or shops selling upholstery fabrics)
- approx. 1.5m (1⅔yd) cotton tape (1.5cm [⅝in]wide)
- Rope (twice the circumference of your circle)
- Sewing thread
- Fabric paint (in a variety of colours)
- Old newspapers
- String
- Drawing pin

preparation

First decide on the size of the playmat. Remember the larger the circumference, the longer the rope handles will be when the mat becomes a bag.

Spread the canvas on the floor, somewhere smooth and clean. To draw the circle you will need a pencil, a length of string, an eraser and a drawing pin.

Make a loop or slip knot in each end of a piece of string the length of the proposed circle's radius.

Put the drawing pin through one loop into the centre of the eraser and slip the other loop over a pencil. Hold the eraser firmly in the centre of the canvas and pull the string taut to form a moveable radius or giant compass. Draw your circle, swivelling the string around the pin as you go. To mark out concentric circles, simply shorten the string in stages.

Cut out, leaving a 2cm (¾in) hem. Press edge over twice, easing the curve in as necessary.

Stitch 1cm (⅜in) in from edge, then top stitch along the very edge for a neat finish. Press.

Cut cotton tape into 5cm (2in) lengths. Fold over in half and overlock or zig-zag cut ends.

Pin loops of cotton tape to hem (see diagram) at 12cm (5in) intervals. Sew backwards and forwards to attach loops securely to the canvas.

painting

Spread old newspapers under the canvas and using fabric paints, work from the inside circle outwards, painting each ring in a different colour. Allow to dry, then fix paint according to manufacturer's directions, usually with a steam iron and pressing cloth. Turn over and repeat for the reverse side with the same design, or something completely different.

assembly

Measure circumference of playmat and cut two lengths of rope this long. Thread the first rope through all the loops so that the ends meet. Bind the ends together firmly with cotton tape and stitch. Begin on the opposite side with the second rope, thread through and bind ends in the same way. Put some toys in the middle and pull ropes in either direction to draw the bag closed. If the ropes are very long, double them over and knot loosely to form a shorter handle.

This basic design could be varied in a number of ways; you could use already printed fabric with a waterproof fabric underneath, or sandwich a circle of wadding between two layers of coloured cotton then quilt the whole playmat in a big spiral…the possibilities are endless!

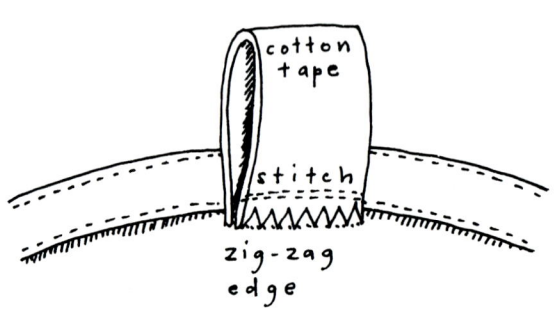

string of toys

This little string of animal faces can be tied over a new baby's cot, or across her pram or car seat. At first she will focus on the brightly coloured shapes, soon she'll learn to recognize the little faces of a dog, a cat, a rabbit and a monkey and before long she'll be swiping them to hear the bells tinkle. I made one for a friend's baby who dragged it around with him long after he learned to walk and often wore it as a necklace.

materials

- 10cm (4in) white felt
- 10cm (4in) red felt
- 10cm (4in) grey felt
- 10cm (4in) yellow felt
- 10cm (4in) pink felt
- 5 large red beads
- 5 medium blue beads
- 5 medium green beads
- (Use wooden or plastic non-breakable beads)
- 150cm (1⅝yd) black cord
- Small amount of polyester stuffing
- Coloured sewing thread
- Black embroidery thread
- 4 small bells

preparation

Trace the patterns onto paper and use as templates to cut two white felt cats, two red felt monkeys, two grey felt rabbits and two yellow felt dogs. In pink felt, cut one monkey's face, two monkey's ears, two rabbit's ears, two cat's ears and three noses.

Sew the monkey's pink face to one red head shape, using pink thread and small neat stitches. In the same way, sew all the animals' respective ears and noses to one of their face shapes. Embroider the face details in black thread, using French knots for the eyes and nostrils and chain stitch for the mouths.

assembly

Wrap tape around the ends of the cord to stop it from fraying. Make a knot about 30cm (12in) in from one end and thread the first three beads (green, red, blue).

Place animal shapes in pairs, with faces on top, and begin sewing together at point A, using blanket stitch in the appropriate colour thread. Stop sewing at B to stuff the lower half of the face, nestling the bell in amongst the stuffing. Place the cord across the middle (between A and B) inside the first animal, then continue to sew around, filling with stuffing as you go. Knot securely before clipping thread to finish.

Thread three beads, then repeat with the next animal and so on until the last three beads.

Arrange animal faces and beads along the cord and tie a knot after the last bead.

french knot - wrap thread around needle twice, reinsert needle at starting position, pull thread taut to finish.

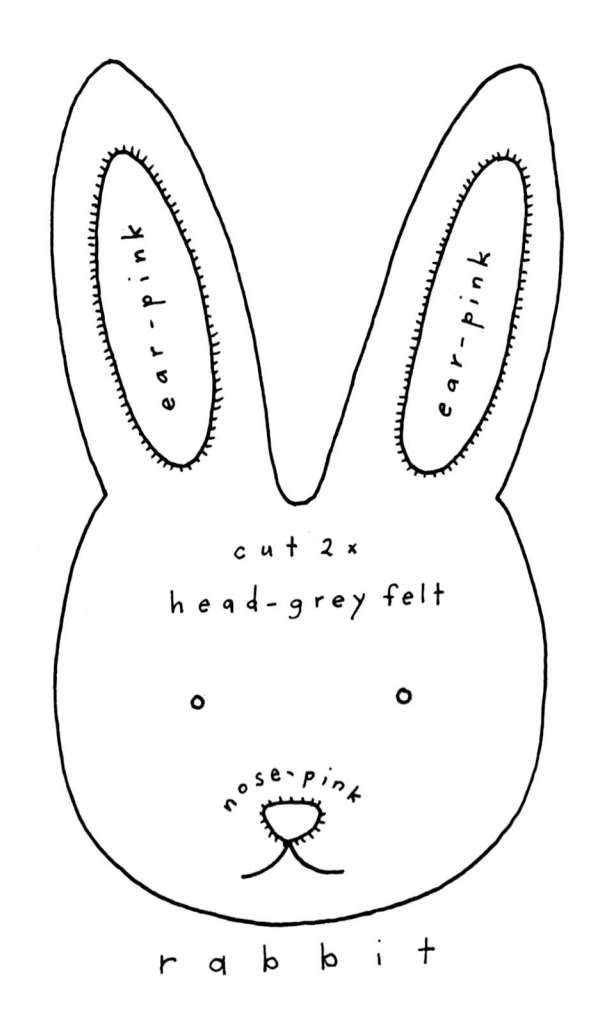

ear-pink ear-pink

cut 2×
head-grey felt

nose-pink

rabbit

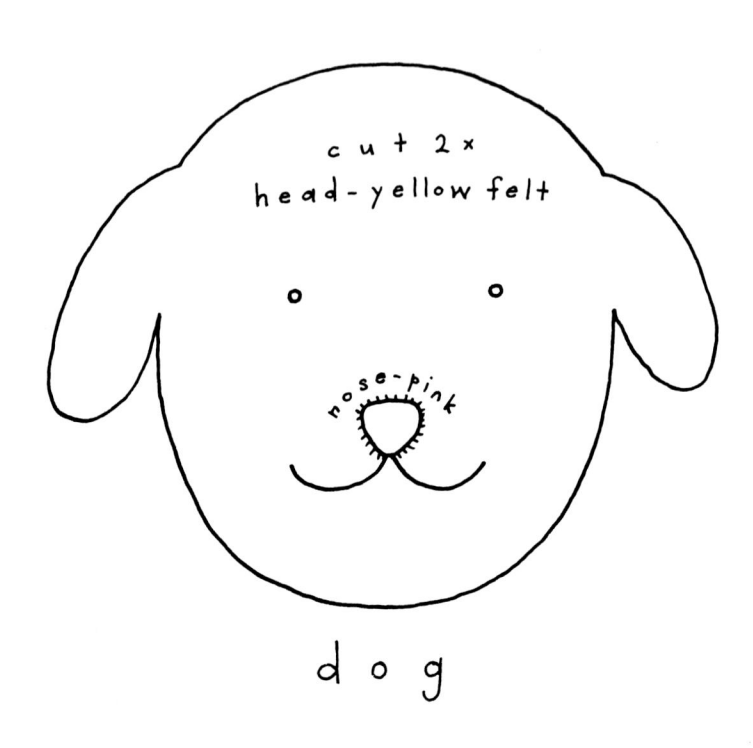

cut 2×
head-yellow felt

nose-pink

dog

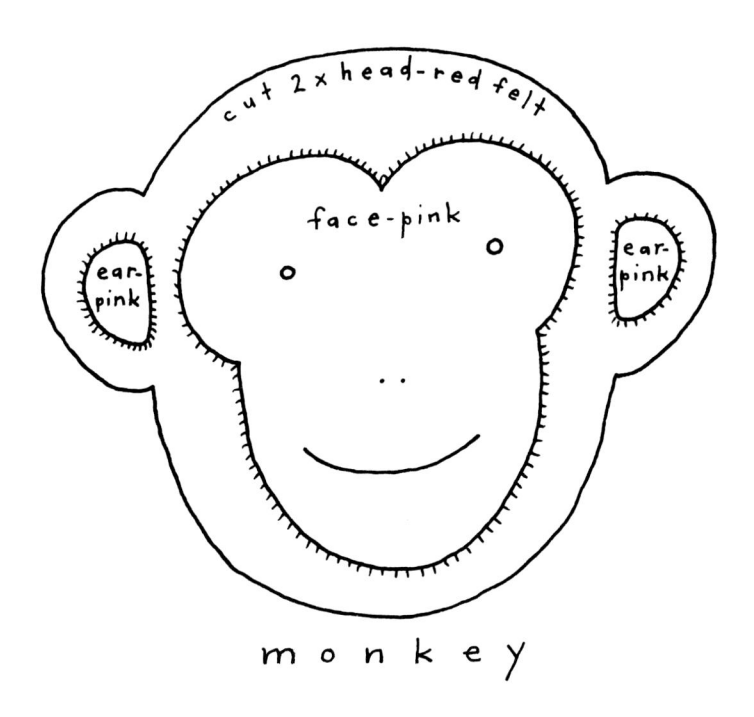

cut 2x head - red felt

face - pink

ear-pink

ear-pink

monkey

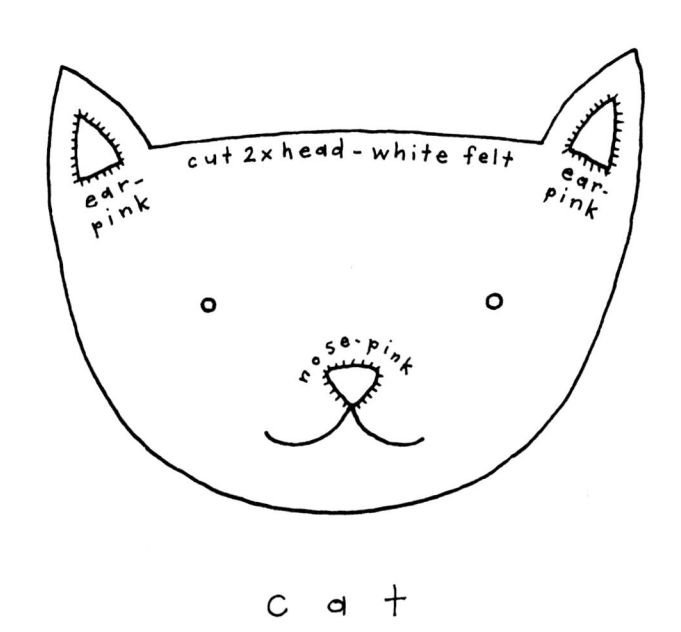

cut 2x head - white felt

ear-pink

ear-pink

nose-pink

cat

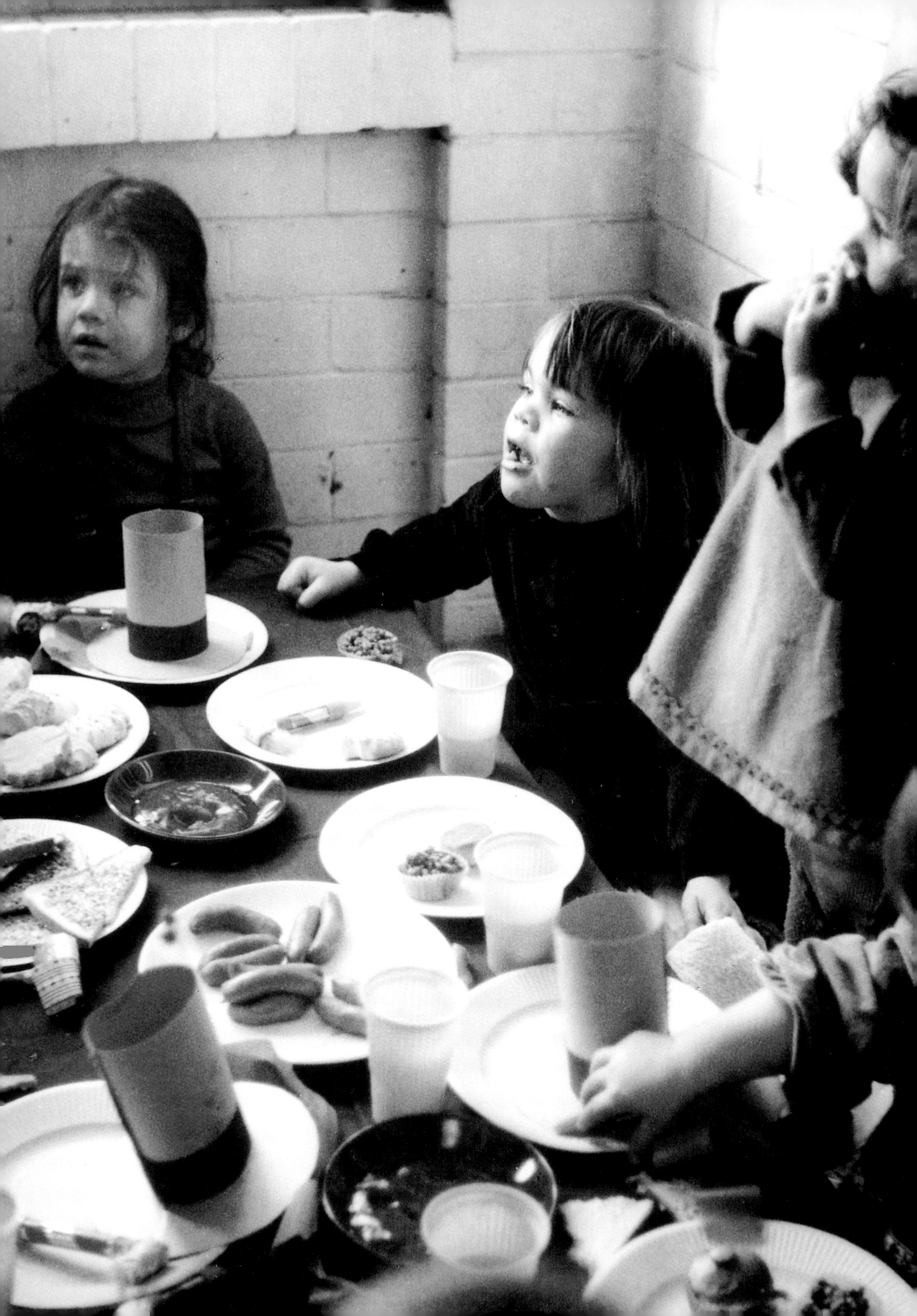

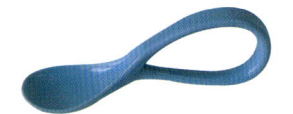

dinnertime

Here we are at dinner time,
Learning to eat with fork and spoon,
Spilling our drinks of orange and lime,
Laughing, shouting, singing a tune.

Martha doesn't like the fish,
Lisa only wants ice-cream,
Zelda tries to swap her dish,
Gregory is in a dream.

There's food on every face.

bright bibs

You can never have enough bibs. These look good, are quite easy to make and, unlike the tiny lace edged ribbon tying ones that don't cope well with a dribble, let alone a mouthful of mush, these are a decent size and therefore useful. They also fasten with Velcro® so you can get them on and off easily. The fruit designs could be replaced with anything you like; a fish, a cupcake, a carrot… or borrow a pattern from one of the other projects; animals or insects, numbers or letters. A custom made bib would be a lovely present. As my daughter is inclined to use her cup as a watering can, I backed some of her bibs with a waterproof layer (see directions below).

materials (for three bibs)

- 40cm (16in) white cotton towelling
- 40cm (16in) white flannel or cotton (or **PVC** for waterproof backing)
- 20cm (8in) orange cotton
- 20cm (8in) yellow cotton
- 20cm (8in) red cotton
- 20cm (8in) pale green cotton
- 20cm (8in) white cotton
- scrap of black cotton
- red, green and blue embroidery thread
- yellow, black, red, pale green, white, brown and orange sewing thread
- 20cm (8in) fusible web
- 3 white Velcro® dots

preparation

With the pattern provided, cut out three bibs from the towelling fabric and three from the flannel backing fabric or **PVC**. Arrange in pairs, pin together and overlock or zig-zag in white thread.

If using PVC, do not sew together with towelling at this stage.

Trace fruit patterns onto fusible web paper.

TIP ✿ Remember that patterns will end up in reverse.

Cut roughly around the paper patterns and, with your steam iron, fuse each to the appropriate coloured fabric. Cut out neatly.

orange: remove paper from the orange segments, arrange on white circle and fuse in position. When cool remove paper from the white circle and fuse in place on the orange circle.

apple: remove paper from white 'centre', arrange on the green apple shape and fuse. When cool remove paper from the green apple and fuse on top of the red apple.

banana: remove paper from black 'ends', arrange them on the yellow banana and fuse in place using a pressing cloth. (Leave banana's backing paper on for the moment.)

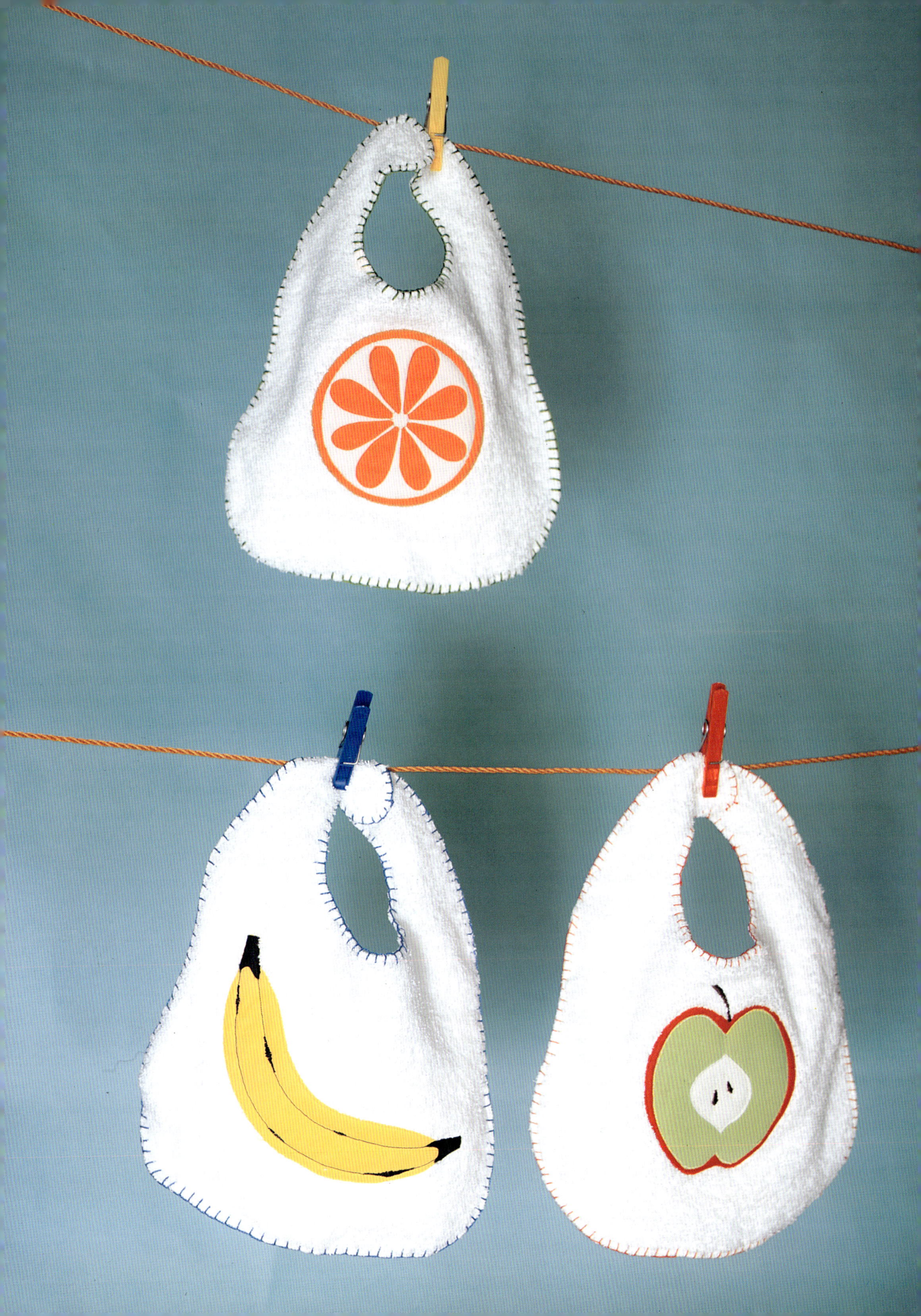

assembly

Remove backing paper from each fruit, position on a bib, cover with pressing cloth and fuse with hot iron. Using a narrow appliqué stitch or close zig-zag (in a small stitch size) in the appropriate coloured thread, sew around each layer of the fruit patterns. Don't forget the apple seeds and stalk in brown thread.

TIP ✿ You can pause and adjust the stitch size on your machine bit by bit to achieve a tapered seed shape or stalk.

If making a waterproof bib, place a piece of photocopy or typing paper behind the towelling when appliquéing, to avoid stretching the fabric out of shape. Just tear the paper away when finished. Then place the PVC behind the bib, pin together and overlock or zig-zag as described above.

Separate Velcro® dots and sew in position on bib ends. The scratchy dot should be sewn on the back of the left bib end, the fluffy dot on the front of the right bib end.

With bright embroidery threads, sew around each bib in blanket stitch to give edges a decorative finish.

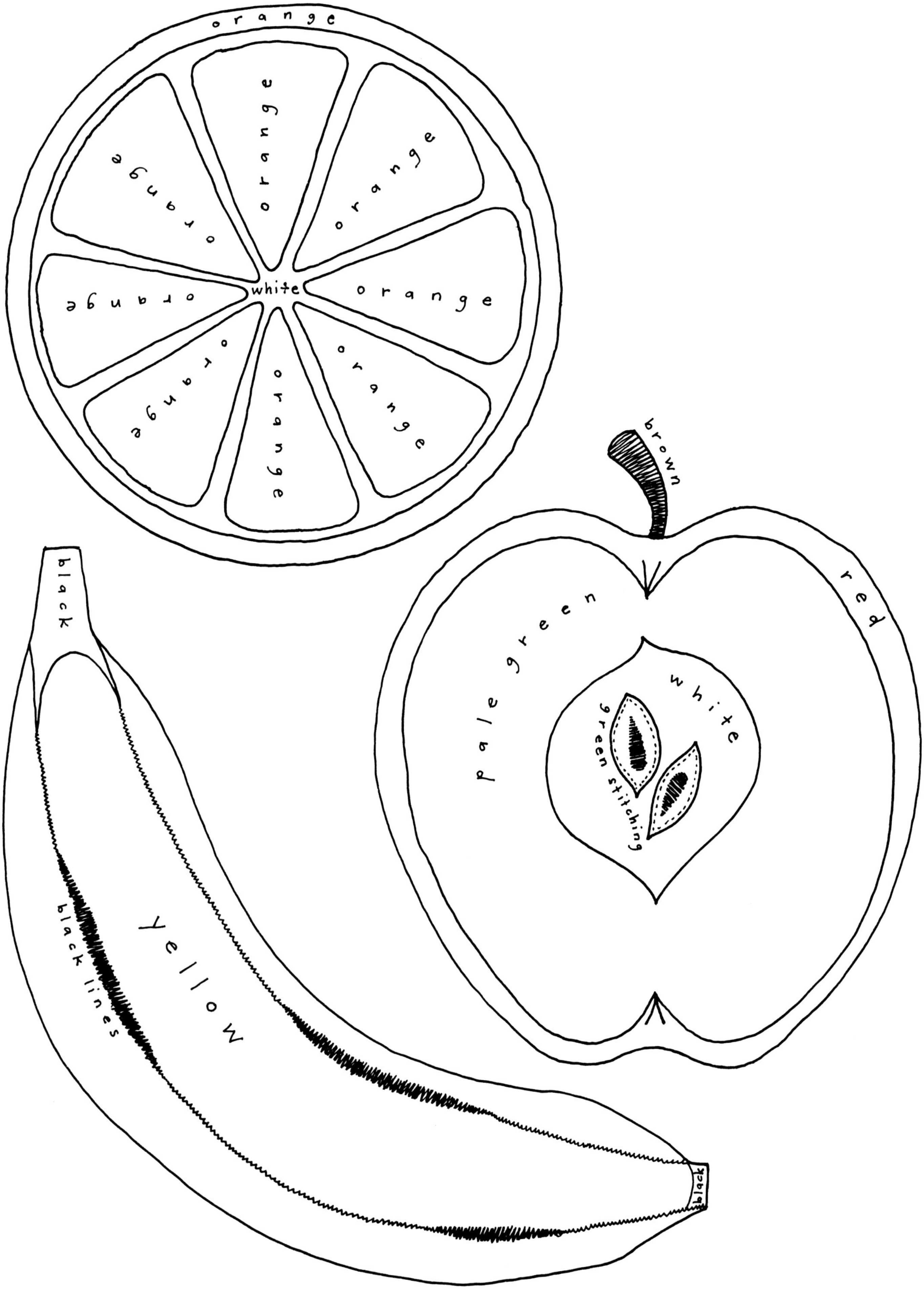

orange
orange
orange
orange
orange
orange
orange
orange
orange
white
brown
red
pale green
white
green stitching
black
yellow
black lines
black

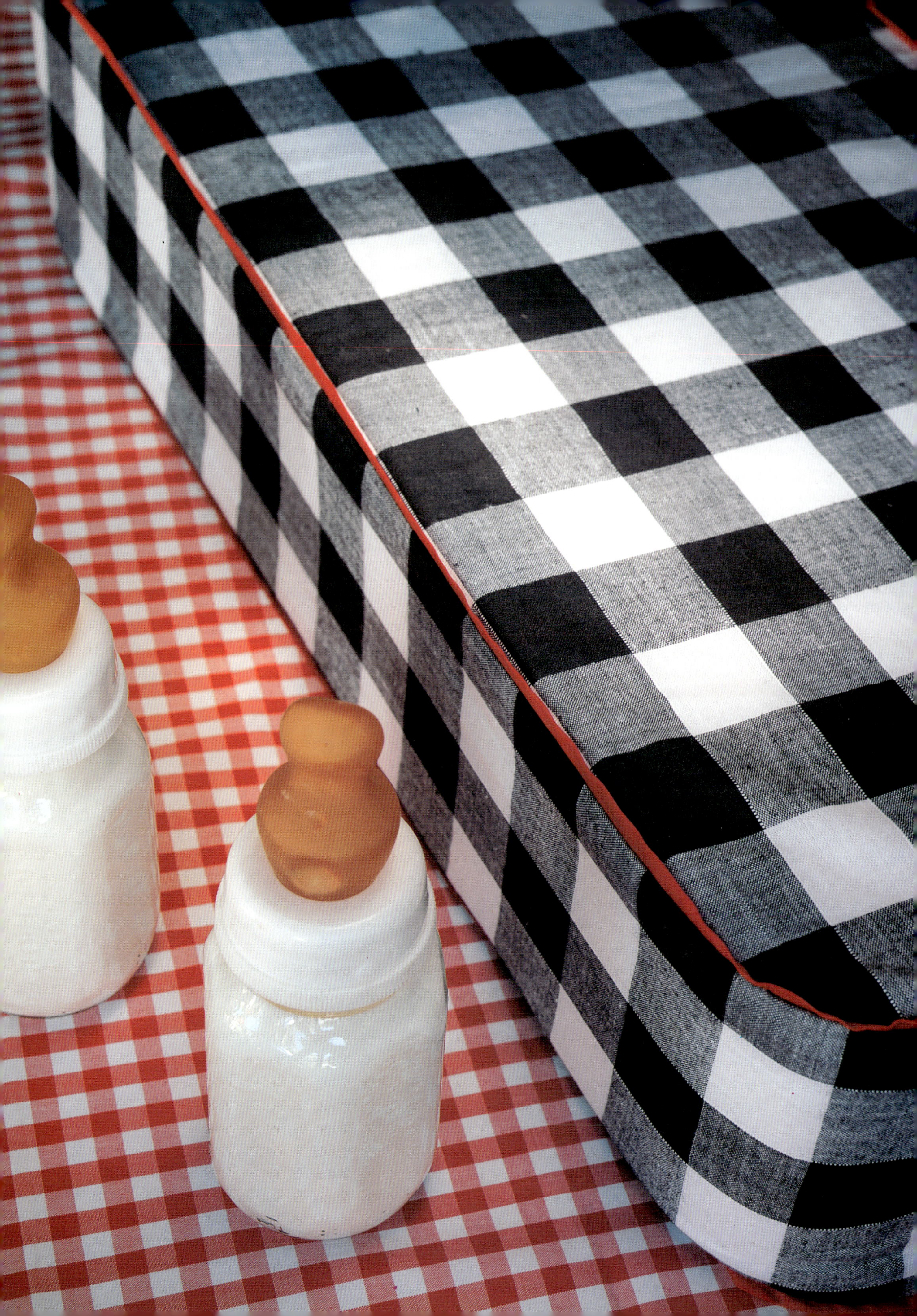

nursing cushion

Feeding a new baby can be a lovely bonding experience; hours and hours to stare at your baby, contemplating her every perfection, trying to ignore the crick in your neck and the ache in your back. Finding a comfortable feeding position and having a good firm cushion to support the baby can make all the difference. Ideally, this cushion should precede the birth, otherwise, in a state of desperation, you'll let any old lumpy pillow or stained cushion cross the threshhold. Make this yourself, get someone to make it for you, or make it for a friend.

materials

- 10cm (4in) thick polyurethane foam cut to size 50cm x 25cm (20in x 10in)
- 1.6m (1¾yd) black gingham
- 3.2m (3½yd) of 3cm (1¼in) wide red bias binding
- 40cm (16in) black dress zipper
- Sewing thread

preparation

Foam is available from specialty shops, hardware stores, and some craft stores. When you buy it, have the corners rounded. Look for offcut bargains.

To make a pattern, trace foam shape onto a piece of paper, add 1cm (⅜in) all the way round for seam allowance. Pin paper pattern to the gingham and cut one piece which will be the cushion top. To make the bottom of the cushion which will incorporate the zipper, you will need to alter the pattern. Fold the original pattern in half lengthwise, then make a second parallel fold 1cm (⅜in) to one side. Cut along this second fold, and discard the smaller piece. Place new pattern on a double layer of gingham and cut out.

For the side of the cushion, cut a strip of gingham 12cm wide x 150cm (5in x 60in) long (this has 1cm (⅜in) seam allowance included). Cut the bias binding into two lengths each 150cm (60in).

assembly

To insert zipper in bottom of the cushion, tack the two gingham pieces together, 1cm (⅜in) in from the straight edge. Mark zipper placement 5cm (2in) from top and bottom. Sew along tack line up to and below the mark only, backstitching for added strength. Press seam open. Fold bulk of fabric to left, leaving right seam allowance extended. Open zipper and place face down with top stop of the zipper at mark, and zipper teeth in line with the seam. Pin in place. Use a zipper foot to stitch along the guideline on the zipper tape. Close zipper and keep pull tab flipped up. Fold bulk of the fabric to the right now, extending left seam allowance. Position the zipper foot to the left of the needle and sew the other zipper tape the same way.

Turn the whole piece of fabric over and spread flat. Top stitch through all layers 6mm (¼in) from seam down the left side, a few stitches along the bottom, then up the right side. Remove seam tacking.

Fold the bias binding in half to make it into a narrow trim, pin to both long sides of the strip of gingham with cut edges together. Tack and remove pins.

Starting on the straight (not a corner) with right sides together, pin side strip to top cushion piece. Begin 1cm (⅜in) in from end of strip to allow for seam.

Sew side strip to the top piece 1cm (⅜in) in from edge, which should allow 5mm (¼in) of binding to protrude to right side. Clip edge of the strip as you turn corners. Join the side seam of the strip. Undo zipper (so you can turn cushion cover through when it is all sewn up). Line up side seam at matching point on the bottom piece (with right sides together) pin and sew in the same way. Turn through to the right side. Compress foam and insert through zip into cushion cover.

Remove cover to wash.

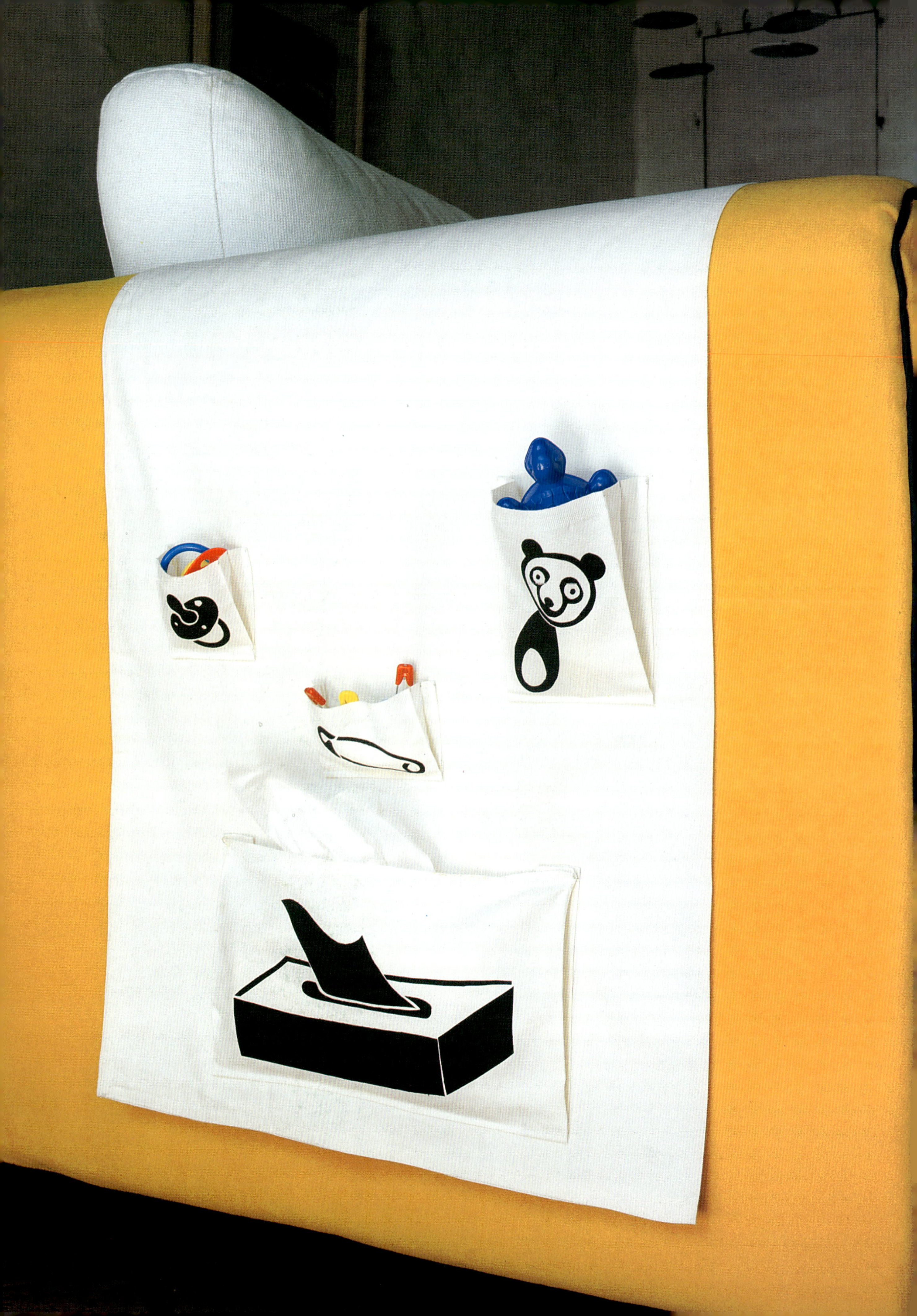

chair holdall

Those first days at home with a new baby often drift by in a milky blur with rounds of visitors, nappy changes and seemingly continuous feeds. I remember taking root in an armchair and barely leaving it all day, getting my long suffering (and very willing) husband to catch and ferry essentials: dribble cloths, tissues, my book, a cup of tea…When he went back to work, I made this handy holdall which kept everything within reach. You could tailor the pockets to suit your needs… you may need a place to put your portable phone, for example, or the remote control. This is a very simple but useful thing to make, and can be adjusted to fit most chairs.

materials

- Cotton canvas (approximately 1.5m [1⅔yd])
- 40cm (½yd) black cotton fabric
- 40cm (½yd) fusible web
- Sewing thread, fabric marker, ruler

preparation

This holdall is a long hemmed rectangle of canvas with pockets at both ends which hang down the side of an armchair. Its middle goes across the seat (or under the seat cushion).

Determine the length of your holdall by following this path with a tape measure. I have made this rectangle 45cm (18in) wide, which should fit most armchairs.

Cut a canvas rectangle 3cm (1¼in) longer and wider than your measurements, to allow for turning edges under.

The pockets are made with an inverted pleat gusset at each side. These side pleats are stitched in place along the under fold, leaving the outer one free. They are topstitched through all layers along the bottom edge.

For the pockets, measure and mark each one onto canvas (see patterns on the following pages for pocket dimensions) remembering to leave at least 15cm (6in) between each for the pleated gussets.

TIP ✿ Align the top of each rectangle with the selvedge, then the tops of the pockets won't need finishing and won't have the extra bulk of a hem.

With marker and ruler add three margins to each side for the inverted pleats and rule guidelines. For the tissue box pocket, the margins are 3cm (1¼in) wide. The bottles, book and rattle margins are 2cm (¾in) wide, and the dummy (pacifier) and safety pin margins 1cm (⅜in). Add 1.5cm (⅝in) to the bottom of each rectangle, to be turned under. Turn each pocket to the wrong side.

Fold in the first margin on each side and press (this is the under fold). Fold back the second margin, press, and the third back in again. Fold up the 1.5cm (⅝in) from the bottom and press again.

Trace patterns onto fusible web paper. Bond web to black fabric using a hot iron, following manufacturer's directions. Cut out the black shapes.

TIP ✿ to align the two baby bottles in adjacent pockets, rule four 2cm (¾in) margins between them. Press a crease along the middle rule and align the two folded inner edges of the pockets along it, so they meet. When you topstitch the pocket in place, simply stitch along the crease line to separate the two pocket areas.

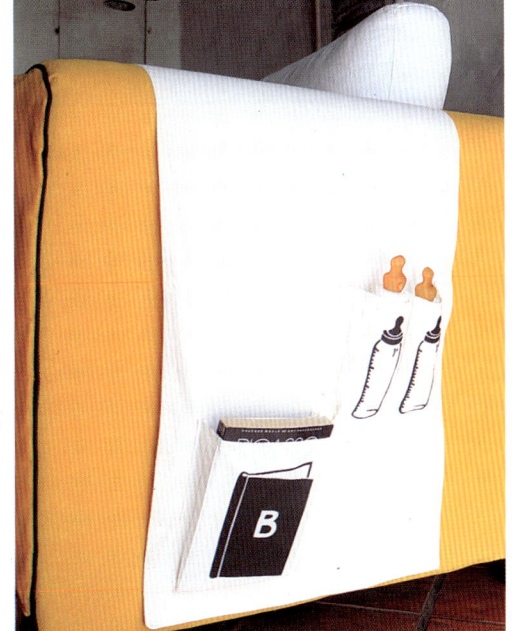

assembly

Press all edges of the holdall under 1.5cm, (⅝in) then under again. Stitch 1cm (⅜in) in from the edge, then top stitch 1mm (1/16in) from the edge for a neat finish. Peel backing paper from the black shapes and position each complete pattern on its appropriate pocket. Using a pressing cloth, fuse each one in place. Decide where you want your pockets for maximum convenience and pin in place.

TIP✿ Arrange holdall in place over armchair before positioning the pockets.

To attach the pockets to both ends of large canvas rectangle, top stitch the under fold of each side only, and across the bottom edge.

As long as all black pieces are properly fused, this holdall should be machine washable.

Pocket dimensions

BOOK ✿ 18cm (7in) wide x 21cm (8¼in) deep
BOTTLE x 2 ✿ 18cm (7in) wide x 18cm (7in) deep
TISSUES ✿ 28cm (11in) wide x 16cm (6⅜in) deep
RATTLE ✿ 10cm (4in) wide x 13cm (5⅛in) deep
PIN ✿ 10cm (4in) wide x 6cm (23/8in) deep
PACIFIER ✿ 7.5cm (3in) wide x 7.5cm (3in) deep

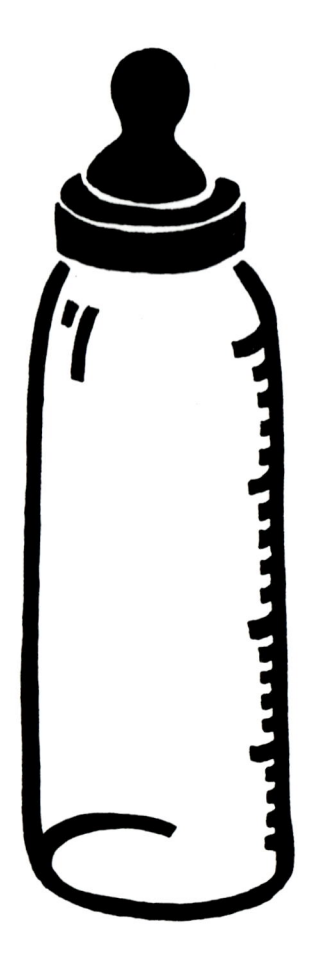

these patterns are ¾ (75%) their original size
enlarge by 133%.

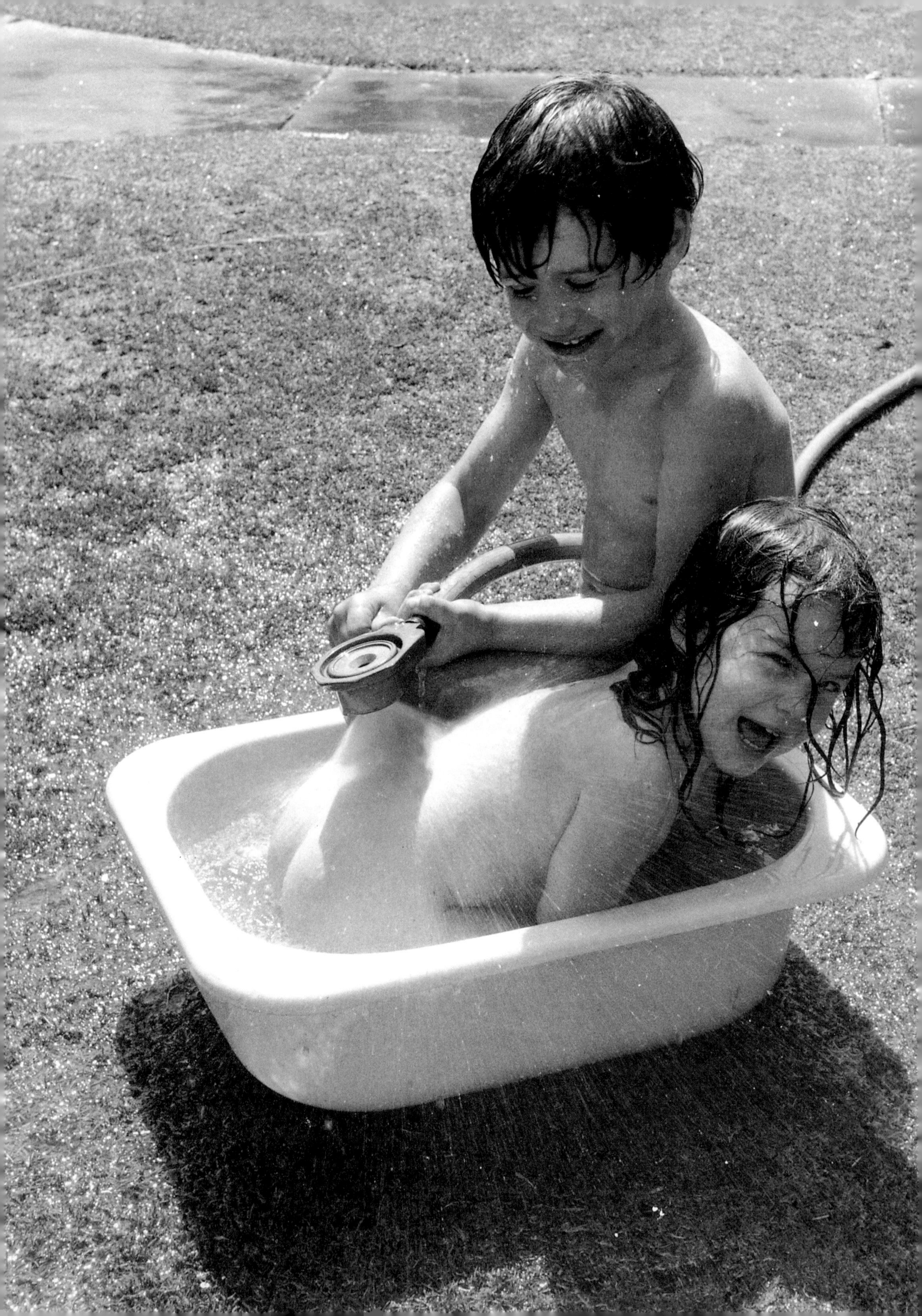

bathtime

Sitting here 'midst soap and bubbles,
Thinking back about the day,
What we thought were fearful troubles
Now have quietly slipped away.

Here it couldn't matter less
If water splashes everywhere.
What always seems an awful mess
Will drain away without a care.

Our ducks and boats and other toys
That clutter up the evening bath
Will wait until tomorrow when
They'll float again and make us laugh.

How nice to be clean once more.

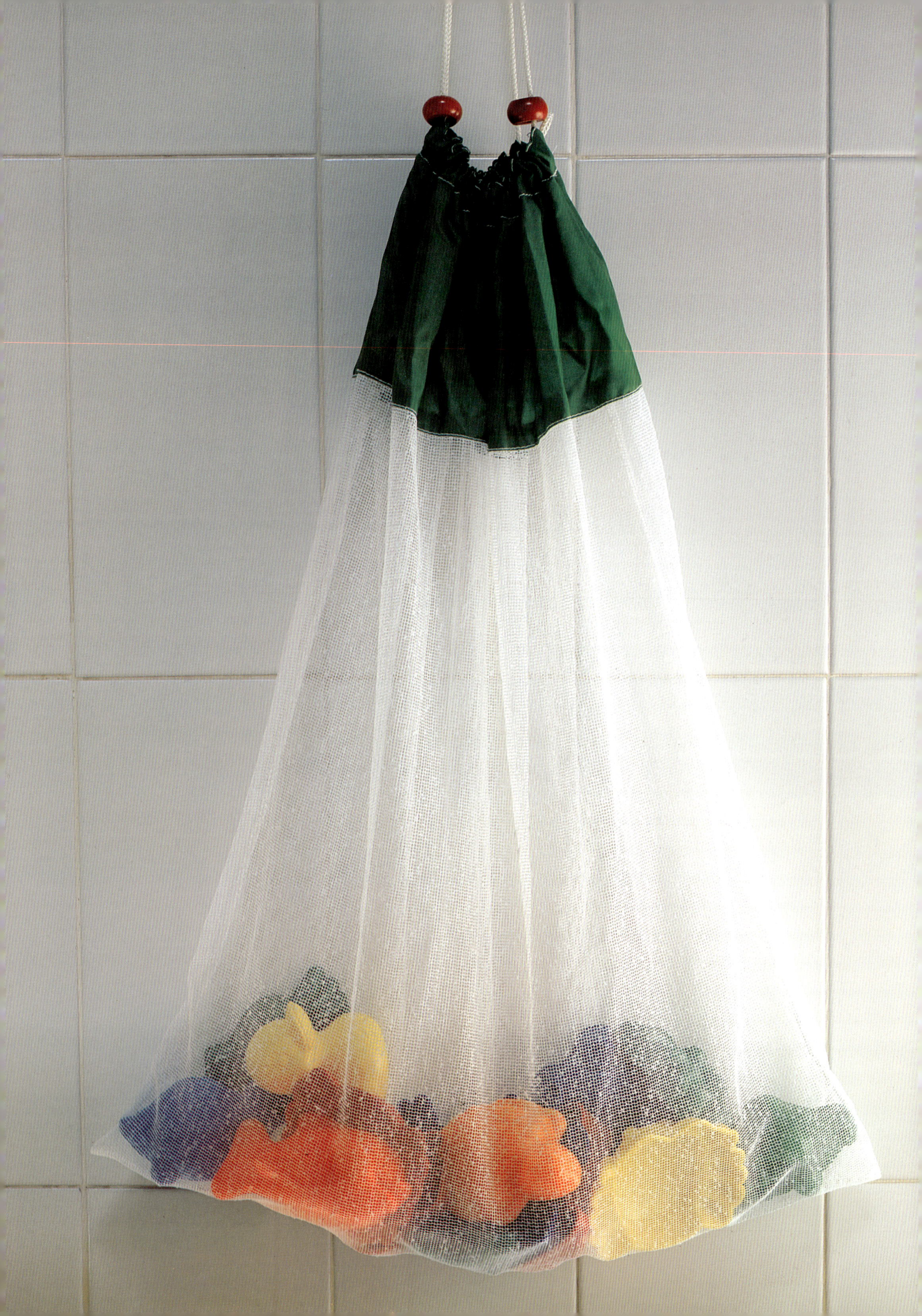

bath toy bag

A lone rubber duck can look innocent enough alongside the soap dish, but when bath toys begin to accumulate, you will soon need something to contain them. This practical draw-string bag is made from nylon net which allows the water to drain away, gives the toys a chance to dry out between baths and makes them less attractive as a bacteria breeding ground (which can't be all bad). Being able to hang the bag out of the way, over a tap or shower head, also reduces the likelihood of accidents caused by grown-ups slipping on a duck. On top of all this, the bath toy bag is extremely simple and inexpensive to make.

materials

- Nylon net cut to size
- 50cm (½yd) coloured 'rip-stop' nylon (the sort of nylon used for shower proof jackets)
- 1.8m (2yd) white nylon cord
- 2 red beads
- Sewing thread

preparation

Measure and cut a rectangle of the net fabric 90cm long x 45 cm wide (36in x 18in).

Overlock (serge) two short edges of the rectangle.

Cut two pieces of rip-stop nylon 48cm wide x 18cm deep (19in x 7in). Overlock (serge) all edges.

Fold one long edge of a piece of nylon over by 2cm (¾in). Fold over again and sew along lower fold to make a casing for the cord. Turn over and top stitch. Repeat for the other piece of nylon.

Cut two pieces of white cord 90cm (36in) long which will be the draw strings of the bag.

assembly

Sew each lower edge of the nylon to one short edge of the net fabric.

To hide the seam edges, fold up towards the nylon. Top stitch along the nylon (from the right side) to keep in place and give a neat finish.

Fold the bag in half with short edges and right sides together. Pin the short sides of the nylon together, and beginning below the cord sleeve, sew down each side 1.5cm (⅝in) from the edge.

Overlock (serge) the net sides together below the nylon. Turn the bag through the right way.

Thread the first piece of cord through one casing, through a bead at the end, then back through the other casing. Knot securely at the end. Thread the second piece of cord in the opposite direction, with a bead at the other end and back through to finish with a knot. Slide the knots of the draw strings inside the casings to hide them.

Open the neck of the bag and use it like a net to scoop up toys out of the bath. Pull the beads to close the drawstrings and the excess water will drain away.

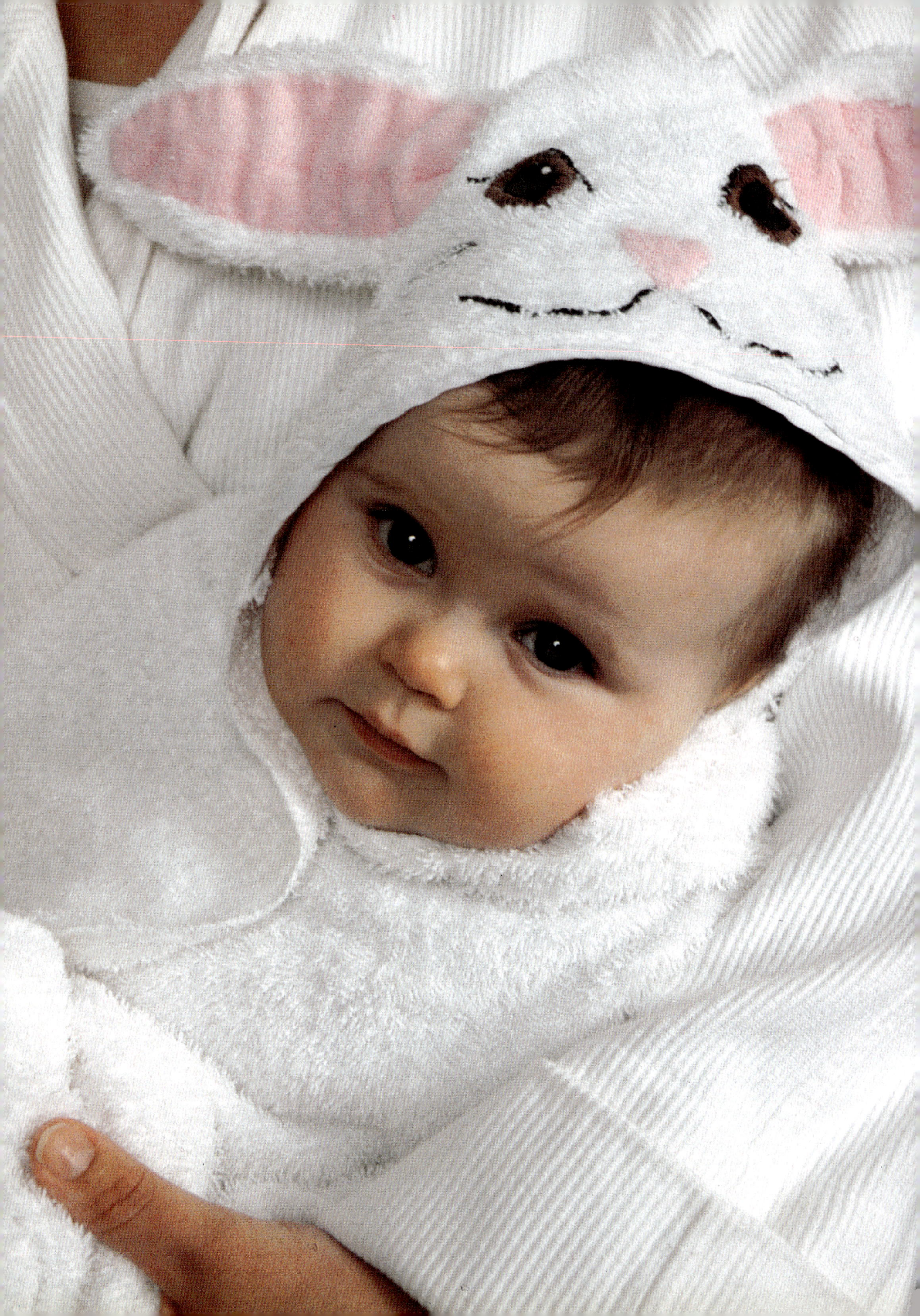

bunny towel

I have to admit this bunny towel leans more towards cute and fluffy than bright and bold, but I've always thought if you can't put rabbit ears on a baby, what's the point of having one? However you could choose to make it with black and white towelling for a bi-colour bunny (I have included a pattern). In years to come I can see the bunny towel doing good service in the dress-up box or as a quick disguise for a teddy bear who wants to hide his true identity.

materials

- 1.3m (1½yd) white towelling
- 10cm (4in) pink towelling
- Scrap of black cotton
- 4m (4½yd) white bias binding
- Black, white, pink and brown sewing thread

preparation

Cut a square of towelling one metre wide. Overlock (serge) all edges.

Pin pattern pieces to leftover towelling and cut one face and four ears. Cut two pink ears, one pink nose and two black circles for eyes.

assembly

Pin a pink inner ear to a white outside ear, sew down first in straight stitch, then around in appliqué stitch or close zig-zag. Repeat for the other pink ear.

TIP ✿ When using appliqué stitch on towelling, place some photocopy paper behind. This will prevent towelling from stretching out of shape.

With pink sides face down, place ears together in pairs of one normal and one pink.

Pin and sew together, leaving lower edge open. Turn both ears through to right side.

Pin black eyes in position on the bunny's face. Using appliqué stitch or a wide close zig-zag stitch, sew just inside the circle in brown thread to form the iris of the eye.

Embroider a white sparkle in each eye with a French knot. (See page 37 for instructions.)

Appliqué the pink nose to the face in pink thread.

Following the guide lines on the pattern, machine embroider (in narrow zig-zag or appliqué stitch) the upper eyelids, mouth and whiskers in black.

Bind the lower edge of face in white bias binding.

Pin ears in position, pink side down, hanging over the front of the face (see diagram).

Place bunny head and ears face down on towelling square. Curve a corner of the towel to match the top of the head. Pin and sew together, overlocking (serging) edges, and turn to the right side.

Bind the edges of the rest of the towel with the remaining bias binding.

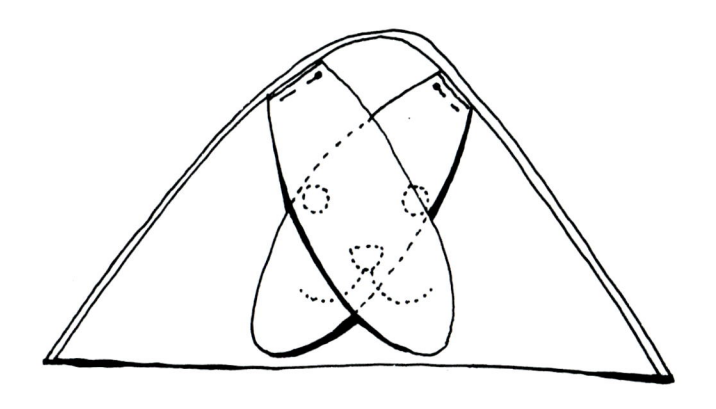

enlarge by 200%.

enlarge by 200%

change mat

You can travel anywhere with this patchwork mat, safe in the knowledge that your baby need never touch the ground! Colourful and quilted for comfort, this change mat folds up into a neat package and has convenient pockets to carry all your nappy changing necessities. Throw it into your bag or under the pram whenever you leave the house, and BE PREPARED!

materials

- Plain cotton fabric in 8 bright colours, approx. 20cm (8in) of each
- 40cm (16in) calico (muslin)
- 40cm (16in) polyester wadding
- 2.5m (2⅔yd) of 5cm (2in) wide red bias binding
- 1 large red button (2cm [¾in] diameter)
- Sewing thread

preparation

Cut patchwork square template from cardboard. Draw around template onto fabric then allow 1cm (⅜in) for seams and cut out squares. Cut 64 squares.

Sew two squares together on drawn lines, then add a third to an outside edge and then another to make a strip of four.

TIP ✿ Follow template lines exactly. This will make it easier to line up squares later.

Choose colours randomly so you have a good mix in each row. Iron as you go, pressing seams open. When you have all your patches in rows of four, divide them into two groups of eight, line them up and sew the long edges together. You should have two patchwork rectangles of eight by four squares to make the front and back of the change mat.

Decide the number and size of pockets you will need. I had three pockets; one for a nappy, one to hold the wipes and one for a tube of cream. Make paper templates to size, trace onto clear vinyl and cut out.

TIP ✿ If the dimensions of your pockets are in multiples of 9cm (3½in), they will line up neatly with the squares of the patchwork.

Position the pockets (I put mine on the back but they could just as easily be placed towards the top on the front). Sew around three sides.

assembly

Cut a rectangle of wadding and one of calico, both approximately 68cm by 34cm (27in x 13½in) or slightly smaller than your patchwork rectangles.

Sandwich wadding between patchwork rectangle without any pockets (right side up) and calico lining. Pin together. Machine quilt along patchwork seams in white thread.

Pin the other patchwork layer to the calico (also right side out) and overlock (serge) or zig-zag all around, curving the corners as you go.

Open out bias binding and beginning just past a corner (this is less conspicuous than starting in the middle of an edge) sew binding to the edge, right sides together with raw edges of patchwork assembly and bias together slightly in from the bias fold line. Fold binding over the edge, turn the mat over, and top stitch the binding down.

Sew a large red button to a point four and a half squares down the centre line on the quilted side.

NOTE ✿ As always with sewing buttons on things for babies, use strong thread knotted securely.

To make a loop for the button, cut an 8cm (3in) piece of bias binding, fold in half, press and stitch down. Fold in half lengthwise and sew ends side by side to the bias binding at centre top (on the non-quilted side).

If you like, you could also make a loop to attach a little toy to entertain your baby during nappy changes. Prepare the binding in the same way then sew one end firmly to the change mat, and attach one half of a press stud to the loop end and the other to the loop base.

To fold up your finished change mat, bring the lower quarter up, fold over again, bring the top row down and pull the loop over the button.

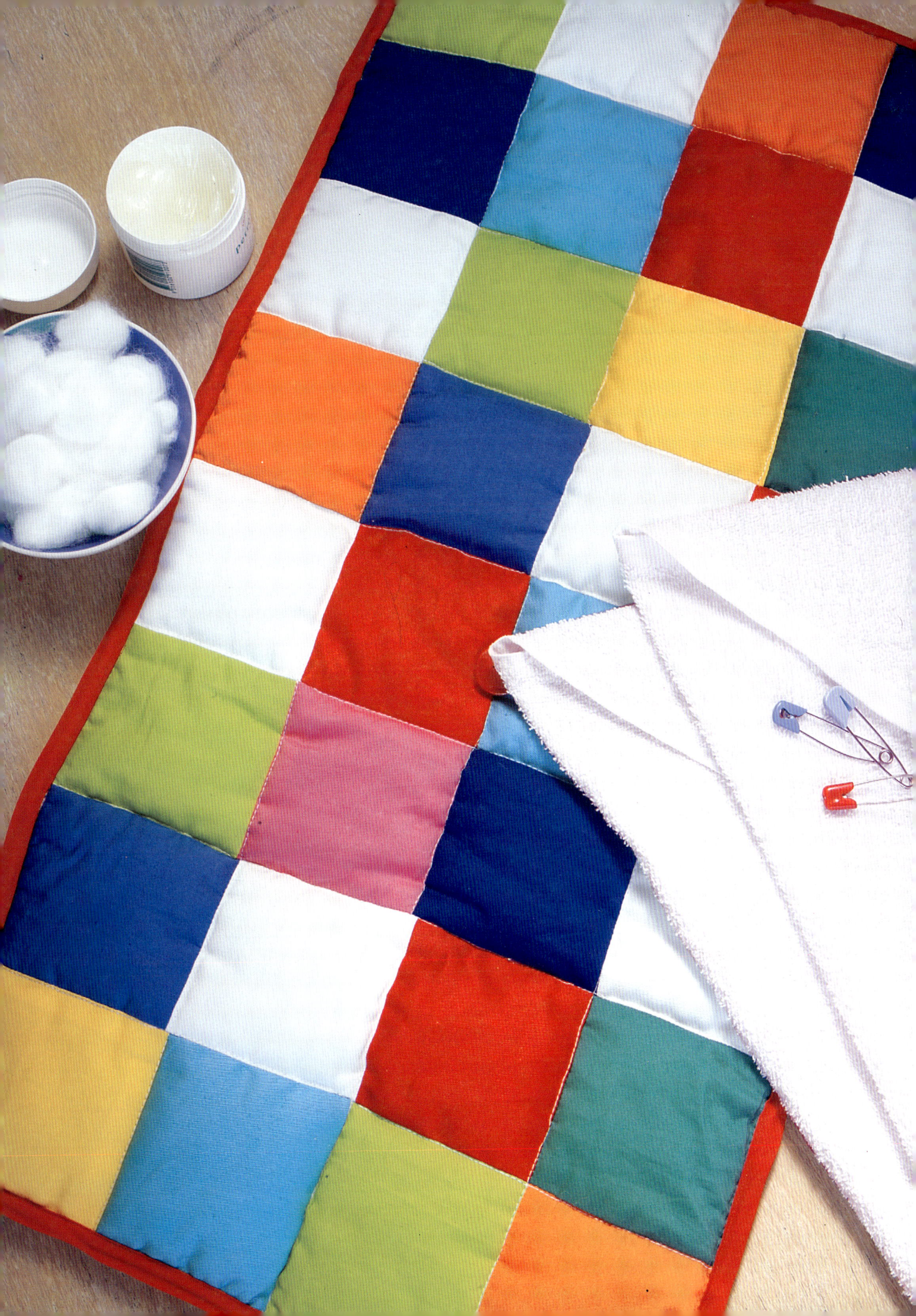

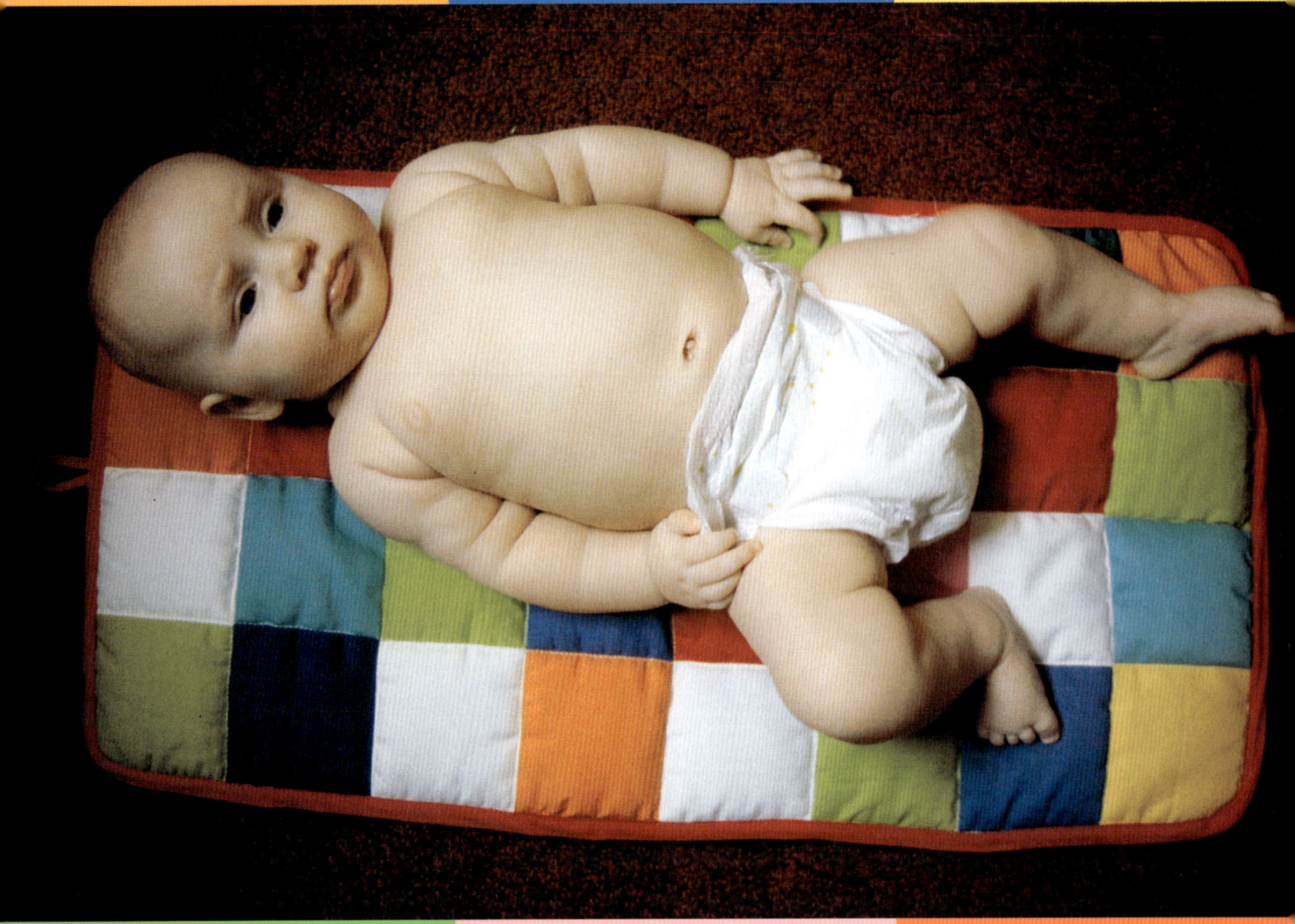

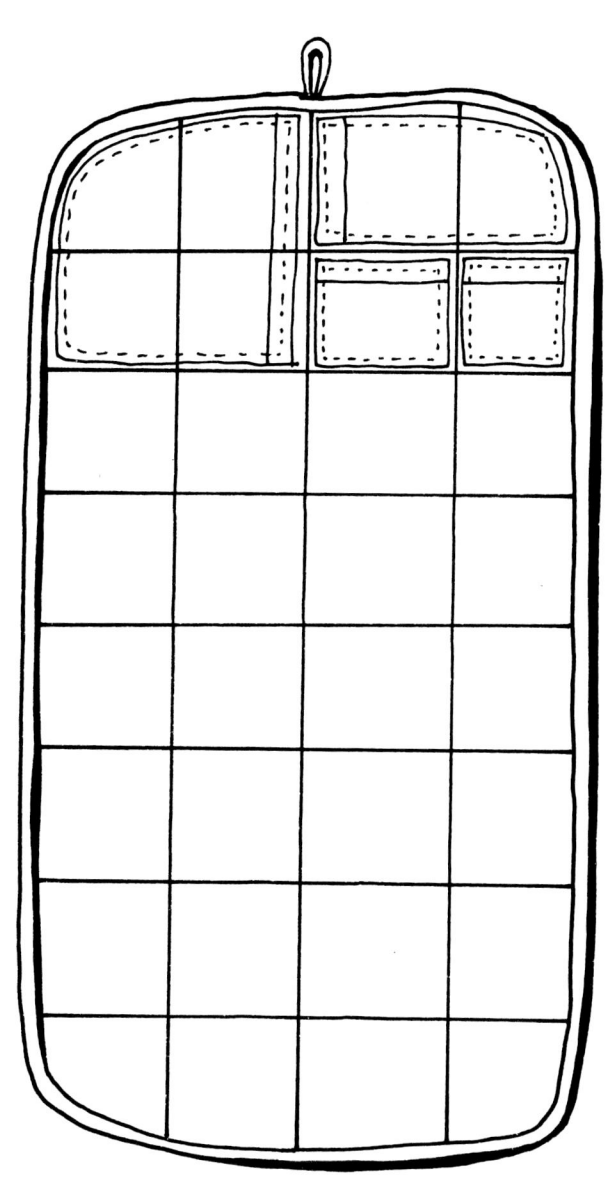

Non-quilted (flat) side has pockets and when rolled up, is on the inside.

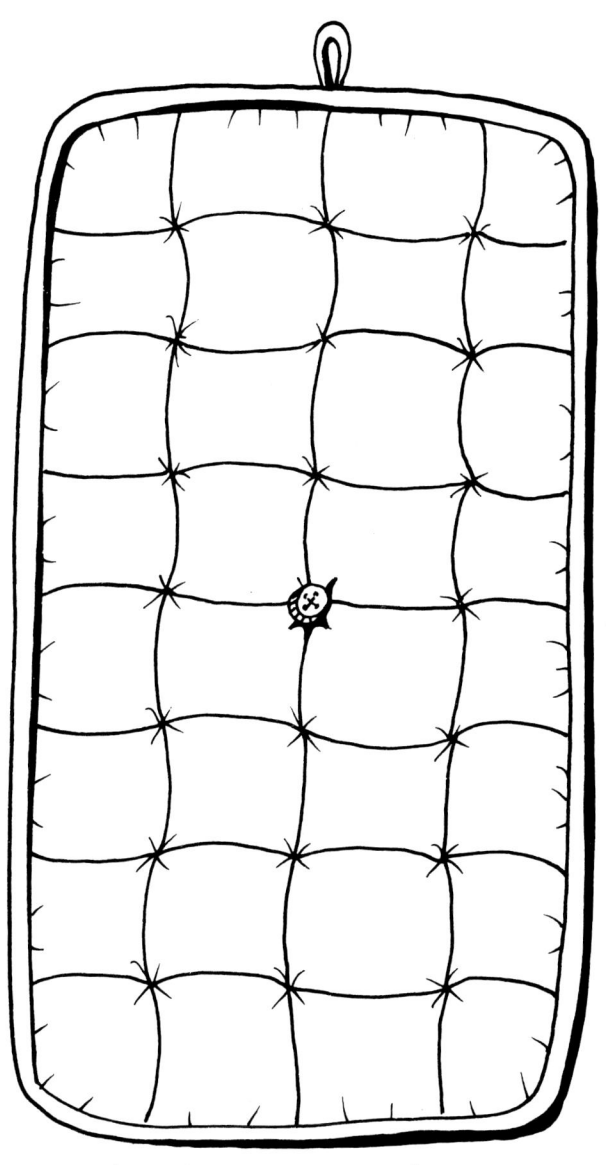

Quilted (puffy) side has the button sewn on. The baby lies on this side.

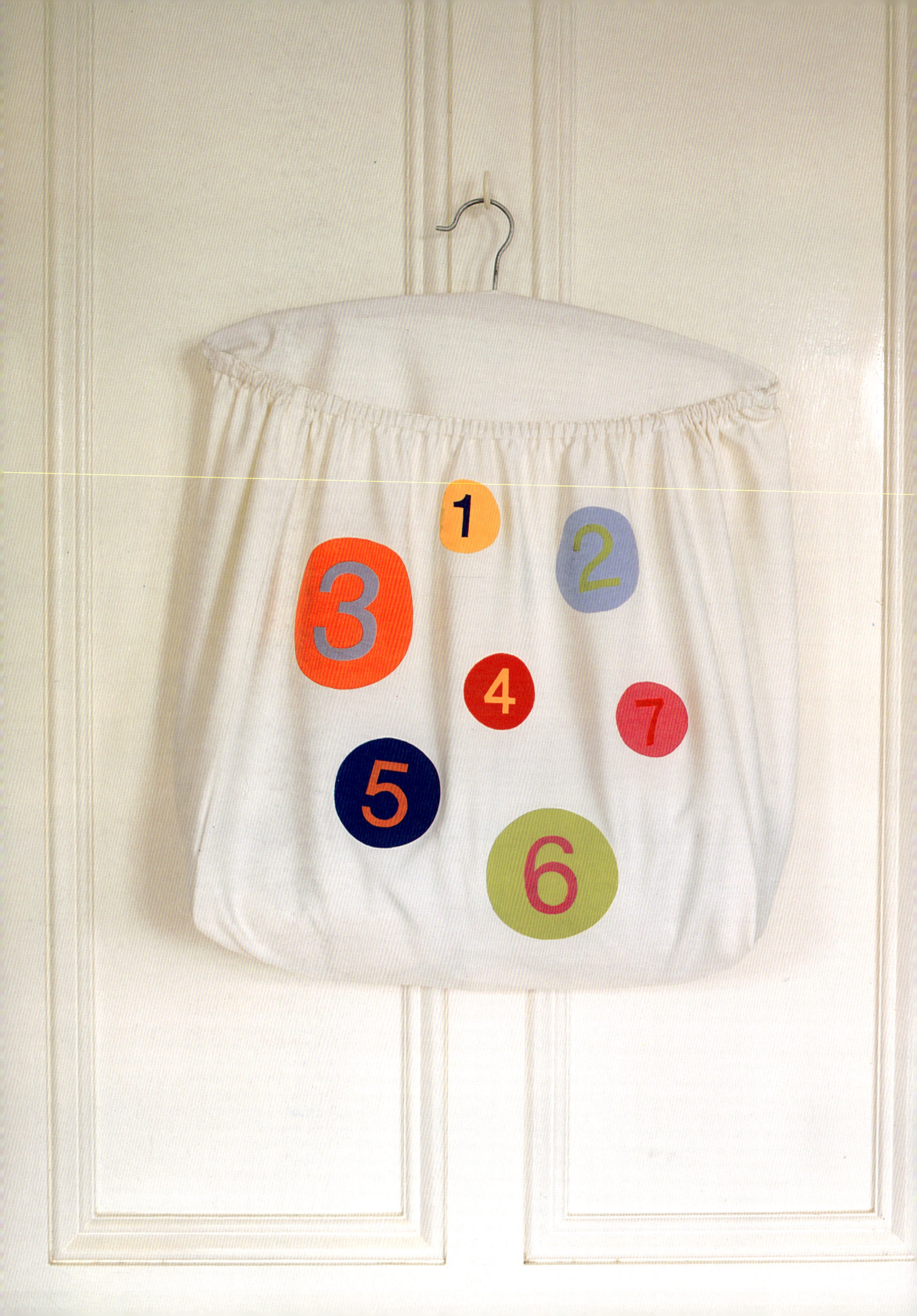
1
2
3
4
7
5
6

clothes tidy

I never imagined a baby could go through so many changes of clothes in a day. We used to have a laundry basket which my very helpful baby would empty regularly, strewing the clothes over the floor and mixing clean ones in with them, so we had the choice of trying to work out which was which, or just washing the whole lot again, either of which took up valuable sleeping time. This out of reach clothes tidy gave us at least an extra twenty minutes a day! It is a simple design, using a wooden coathanger as a frame to support the bag and as a means of suspending it. The coathanger can be removed whenever the bag needs washing.

materials

- 1m (1yd) white cotton drill
- Wooden coathanger
- Coloured cotton scraps
- 20cm (8in) fusible web
- 30cm (12in) of dressmaking elastic
- Sewing thread

preparation

Trace the circles and numbers onto the fusible web paper (remember they will come out in reverse). Cut roughly around each circle and number pattern. Apply each pattern to a piece of coloured fabric, following the guide or choosing your own colours, and fuse according to manufacturer's directions (usually by pressing with a hot iron for several seconds). Neatly cut out each circle and number.

To make the bag, you will need to cut four rectangles. For the back, base and front of the bag, cut one rectangle 40cm wide x 95cm (16in x 37½in) long. For the lining, make one rectangle 40cm wide x 35cm long (16in x 14in), and for the side panels, two rectangles 18cm wide x 37cm long (7in x 14½in).

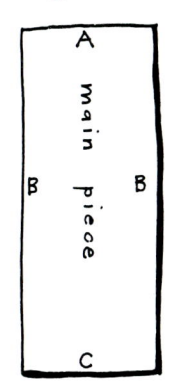

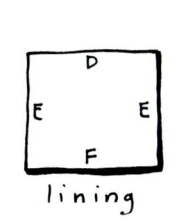

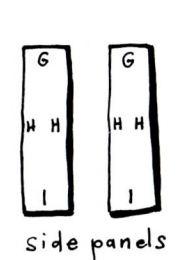

assembly

Pin the long edge of the lining (D) to the short edge of the main piece (A). (See diagram below)

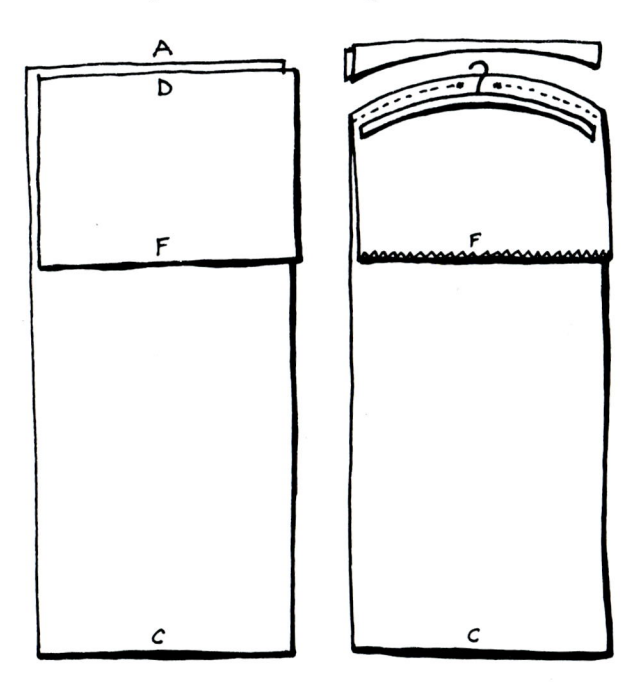

Place coathanger 1cm (⅜in) from the top edge and trace its curve onto the lining. Mark an opening where the hanger protrudes. Sew along this curve up to the mark and beyond the mark, backstitching on either side of the opening for strength. Trim 1cm (⅜in) above stitch line, clip curve if necessary, press and turn to right side.

Finish lower edge of lining (F) by overlocking (serging) or hemming.

Put a safety pin in one end of the elastic and attach the other end to the edge of the bag with an ordinary pin. Thread the elastic into the casing, gripping the safety pin through the fabric and pushing it forward, gathering up the casing as you go. Make sure you don't lose the other end or you'll have to begin again! Sew elastic to attach firmly at either end to finish.

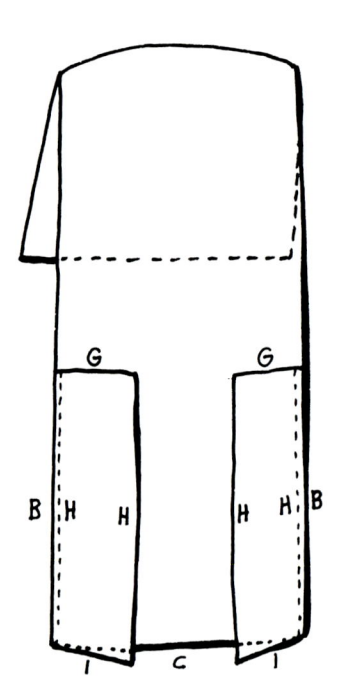

Pin long edges of side panels (II) to the back of the main piece (at lower B). (See diagram above) Sew side seams, open flat and press.

Turn the whole assembly to the other side and fold the lower edge (I+C+I) up 1.5cm (⅝in) then up again to form the casing for the elastic. Press and sew close to fold. Turn to right side and top stitch close to the edge.

Arrange coloured circles on the main panel below the casing. Edge C is now at the top.

Remove backing paper and with an iron and pressing cloth, fuse circles in position on the front of the bag.

Turn upside down again, and continue to pin the short edges (G) and other long edges (H) of each side panel to the main piece (B).

TIP ✿ You will need to clip the edge of the main piece to allow it to turn a 90° corner around the side panel.

Sew the side panels to the main piece (clipping at corners) and finish all edges (except casing which must be kept open for the elastic).

Turn bag out the right way and insert coathanger under the lining, threading the hook through the small opening in the top.

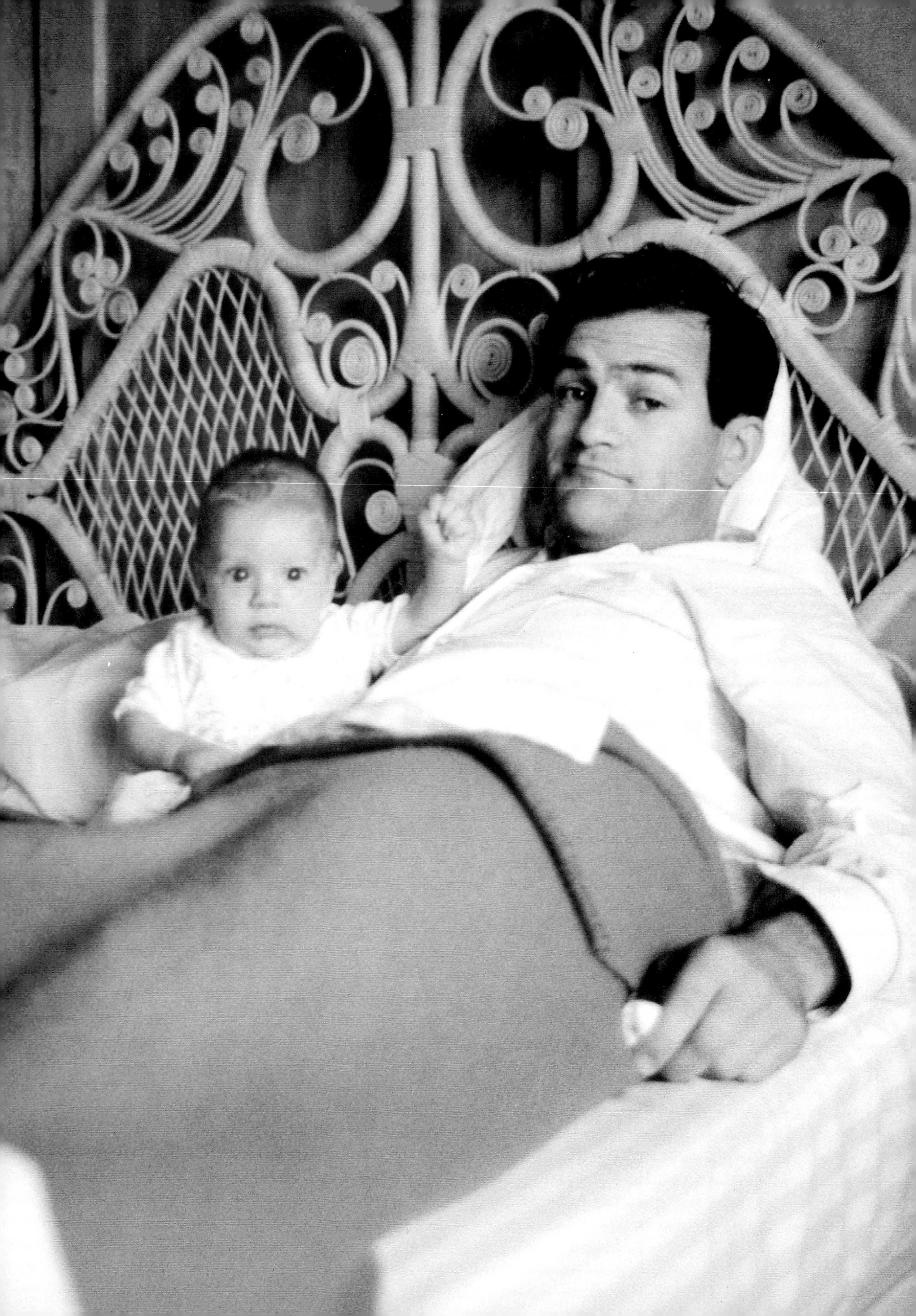

bedtime

I'm ready now for story time
With favourite books beside my bed.
Daddy reads slowly line by line
As if to store them in his head.

There's Humpty Dumpty, Mother Goose
And giants and kings and queens and elves.
There's Peter Rabbit and Dr Seuss
And more books waiting on the shelves.

I'm drifting off to slumberland
Two lips have touched me on the cheek.
Still holding Teddy by the hand
I cannot stop myself from sleep.

Tomorrow is another day.

jigsaw cushions

This cushion puzzle is bright and decorative, irresistible to toddlers and it is much admired by adults. Our set of cushions has managed to work its way onto the sofa! When not in use, the cushions can be neatly stacked in a corner. They can be made with or without the piping.

materials

- Piece of 2.5cm (1in) polyurethane foam 30cm x 90cm (12in x 36in)
- 50cm (20in) red cotton drill
- 50cm (20in) blue cotton drill
- 50cm (20in) yellow cotton drill
- Polyester wadding
- Sewing thread

preparation

Trace the jigsaw patterns onto 2.5cm (1in) thick foam. Cut them out with scissors. Designate each one to a different colour.

assembly

Fold the fabric pieces in half and trace the jigsaw patterns onto their respective colour of cotton drill. Cut out through both layers (making two pattern pieces), adding 1.5cm (⅝in) seam allowance.

To make the side edge for each cushion, cut a strip of fabric 8cm (3¼in) wide by 142cm (56in) long. Make piping twice the length of the strip.

Pin piping along both long sides of the strip, with raw edges together. Sew with the zipper foot.

TIP ✿ To ensure a neat finish, pull out the last 1.5cm (⅝in) of cord from the piping, and snip off, allowing cord to retract. (This reduces bulk in the side seam)

With right sides together, sew the two ends of the strip to form a band. With raw edges outward and right sides together, pin one edge of the band along the traced outline of one cushion shape, clipping the seam allowance of the band where necessary to follow outward and inward curves.

NOTE ✿ The stitching lines must match, not the outside edges.

Sew the other side of the jigsaw to the band in the same way, leaving a 20cm (8in) opening on one of the straight sides, rather than at a protruberance.

Turn through to the right side. Roll up the appropriate foam jigsaw piece and ease into the opening, unrolling and smoothing into place. This gives the cushion its shape.

Now fill the rest of the cavity with the wadding, but do not overstuff, as your jigsaw cushions will bulge and be difficult to fit together.

Sew up the opening by hand to finish. You can press the finished cushion if you like.

The foam layer gives a neat flat surface that is the upper side of the jigsaw cushion.

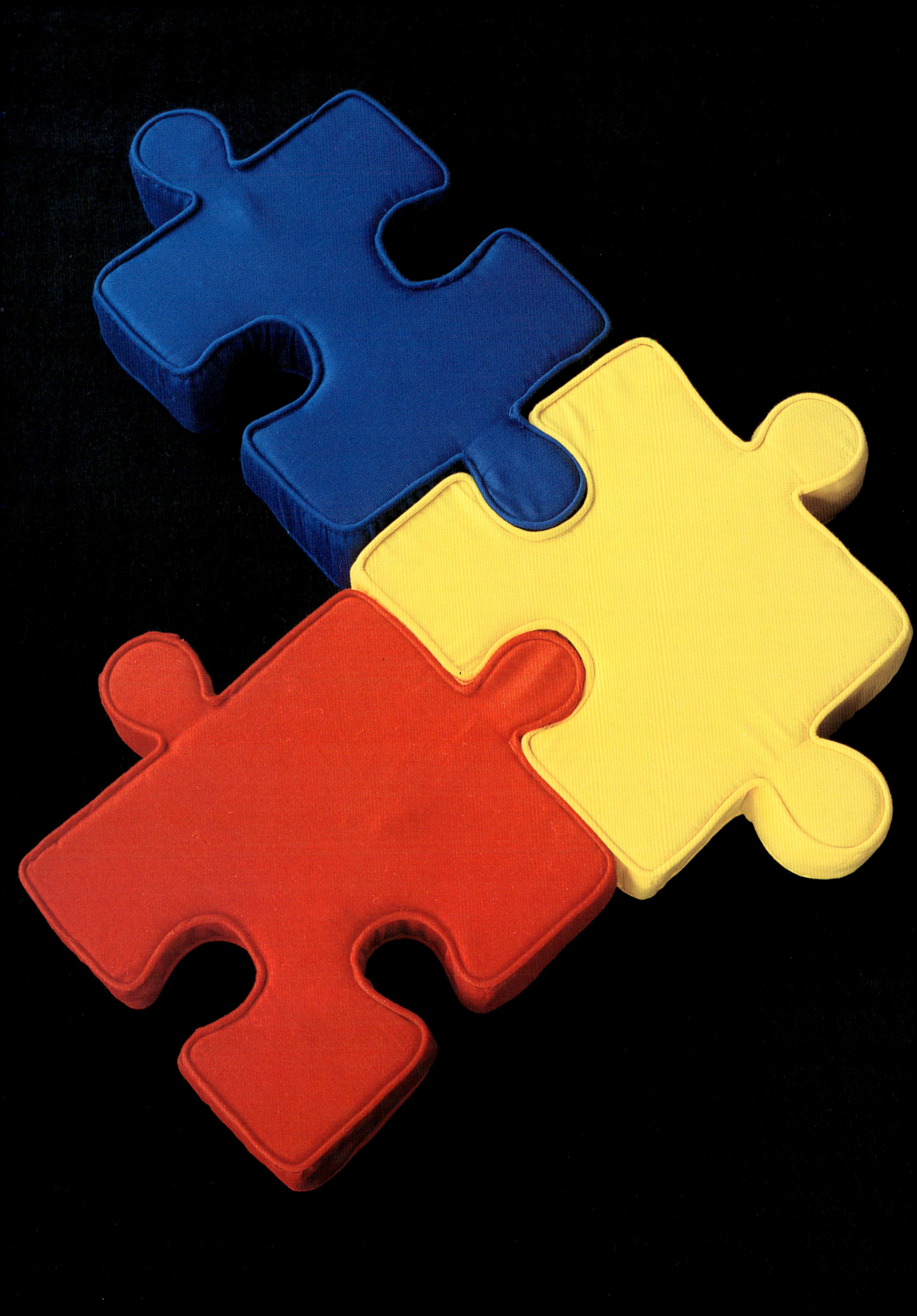

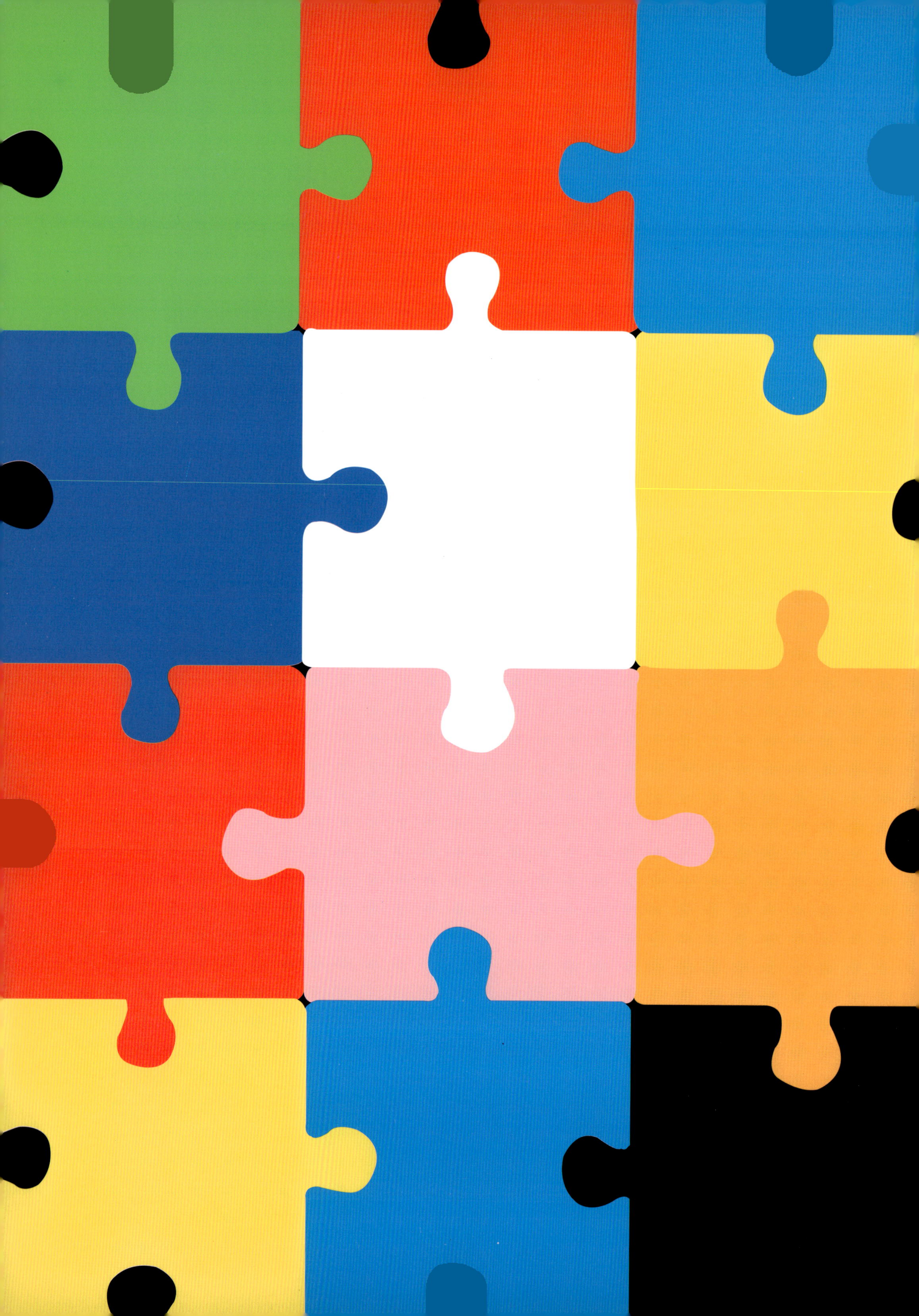

enlarge these patterns by 200%.

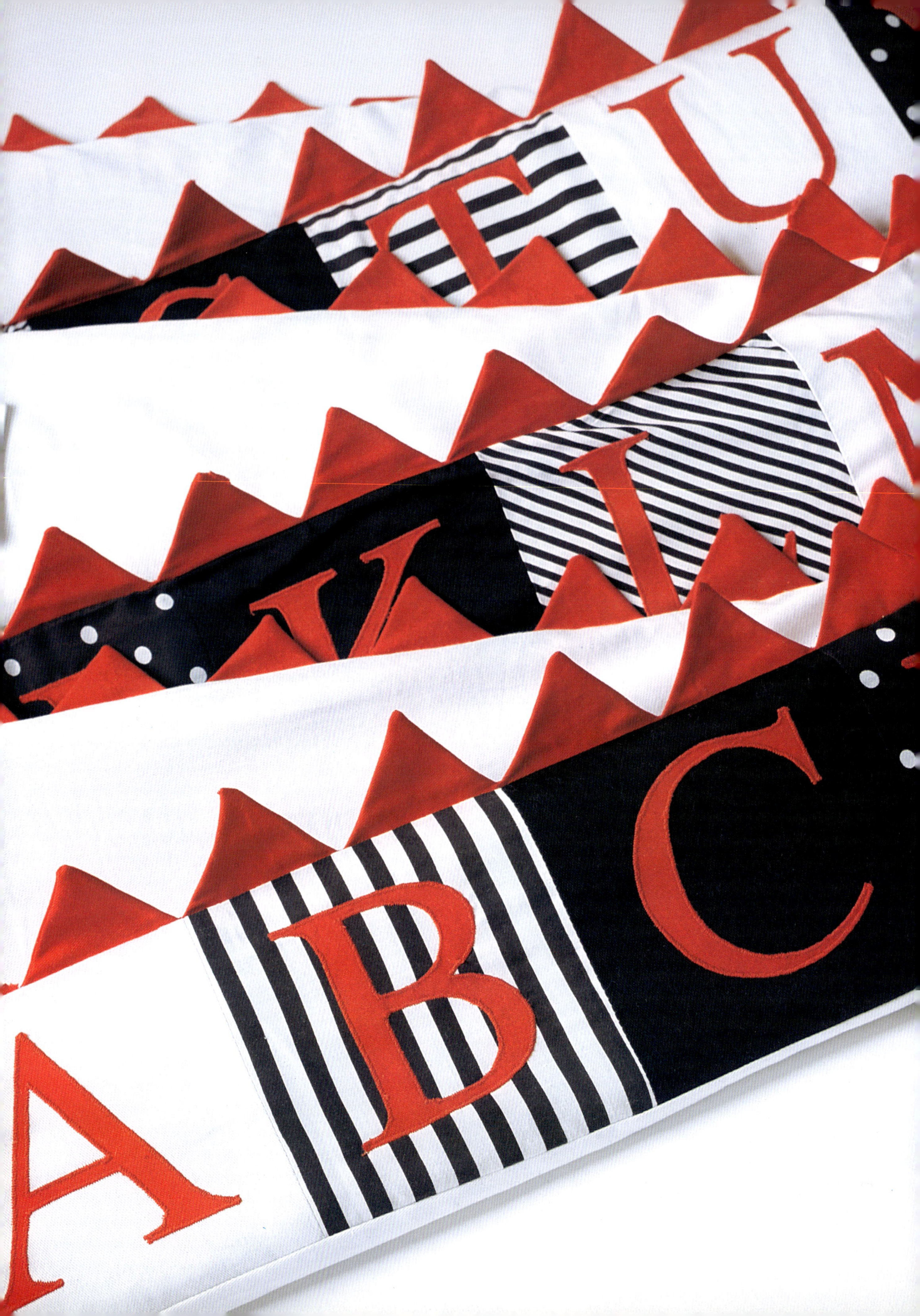

alphabet bumper

Considering that a baby must spend an awful lot of time staring at the bumper on his cot, it might as well be interesting (not to mention bright, bold and educational). This padded cot bumper protects the baby from bumping its head, or getting arms or legs stuck through the bars or railings. It is made with black and white patterned fabrics to stimulate the newborn, and has large, red appliquéd letters for the older baby. You never know, with the alphabet being the last thing he sees at night and the first thing he sees in the morning, your baby might be reading at one!

materials

- 2.5m (2⅝yd) white cotton drill
- 100cm 1(yd) black cotton drill
- 2.5m (2⅝yd) red cotton drill
- 70cm (¾yd) black and white striped fabric
- 70cm (¾yd) black and white spotted fabric
- 70cm (¾yd) black and white diagonally striped fabric
- 2.5cm (1in) thick foam cut to size (see **preparation** for measurements)
- red and white sewing thread
- 1.5m (1⅝yd) fusible web
- Contact adhesive (rubbery, slightly sticky glue)

preparation

This cot bumper sits above the mattress and runs around the inside of the cot. It is held in place with cotton tapes which tie onto the bars at intervals. As cots come in different sizes, you may have to adjust this pattern to suit your needs. It is fairly simple to work out, but if you have an unusually shaped cot you may need to apply some mathematics.

First measure the width and length of your baby's cot. Add the two figures together and double the amount to arrive at the perimeter measurement.

Divide this number by 26 (the letters of the alphabet) to calculate the dimensions of each square.

NOTE ✿ You should be able to fit nine squares along the long sides and four along the short sides. Don't worry too much if it doesn't work out to the very last millimetre.

In my case, the width of the cot was 56cm (22in) and the length was 126cm (50in) which is a fairly standard size. Added together and doubled this makes a perimeter of 364cm (4yd). Divided by 26, meant that each alphabet patch was 14cm (5½in) square.

After calculating this figure, make a square template to size from a piece of cardboard.

Using an erasable marker draw around the template onto white cotton drill and cut out, leaving a 1.5cm (⅝in) border all around for seam allowance. Repeat until you have seven white squares. In the same way, prepare six black squares, four vertical stripe squares, five spotted squares and four diagonal stripe squares (or whichever patterns you have chosen).

Enlarge alphabet by approximately 400% (so that each letter fits into your square) on a photocopier. Trace each letter onto fusible web (remember they will come out in reverse). Apply fusible web to red cotton drill, following manufacturer's directions (usually with a hot iron). Cut out around each letter.

Follow the diagram below to allocate each letter the correct background fabric.

Cut a strip of foam the same net width as the squares, but without seam allowance.

Divide into four pieces; two the length of the cot, and two the width of the cot.

To prepare the back of the bumper, use these foam pieces as templates to trace onto white cotton drill, adding 1.5cm (⅝in) seam allowance to all sides, and cut out.

Prepare a long strip of red cotton drill, 16cm (6¼in) wide by the total length of the bumper.

TIP ✿ You will probably need to make two strips and join them together with a centre seam.

Fold over in half lengthwise and press.

Make a cardboard template of the triangular points, (200% larger than the the pattern on page 77). Trace and repeat this pattern right along the strip. Sew along this zig-zag line and trim to 5mm (¼in) above stitch line. Clip into valleys and trim extreme points off mountains. Turn right side out and press.

assembly

Peel the backing paper from each letter and fuse in position on the appropriate square.

TIP ✿ Rotate the patterned fabric for variation, as indicated in the diagram on the previous page.

Machine appliqué the letters in red thread.

With letters the right way up, place 'B' face down on 'A', pin and sew the right hand sides together along trace line, 1.5cm (⅝in) from the edge. Open out the seam and press flat.

In the same way, sew 'C' to 'B' and so on through the alphabet.

Pin the white rectangles together by the short side edges, alternating short and long. Sew the side seams, open out and press flat. Flip the whole strip over to the right side. Cut the cotton tape into six 30cm (12in) lengths, and sew each piece to the white strip at seams (which will be corners) and in the middle of each long side.

Pin red bunting strip along the top of the front of the alphabet bumper, with cut edges together and points down. Place white strip face down over the top, and line up edges. Pin and sew top and strips together. Press and turn through to right side.

Insert foam rectangles between bumper front and back, through the open edge.

TIP ✿ The foam will sit more neatly if it has tapered edges. There is a simple trick to this. Squeeze contact adhesive (see materials) along one edge. Make an inverted pleat in this edge, pinching the sides together. The glue is very tacky and will hold immediately. Repeat edge by edge.

Top stitch the lower side closed, folding in cut edges by 1.5cm (⅝in). Top stitch corner seams through both thicknesses (from the right side) to keep each piece of foam in its correct compartment. Install the bumper, tying cotton tapes around the bars of the cot in six places to keep it in position.

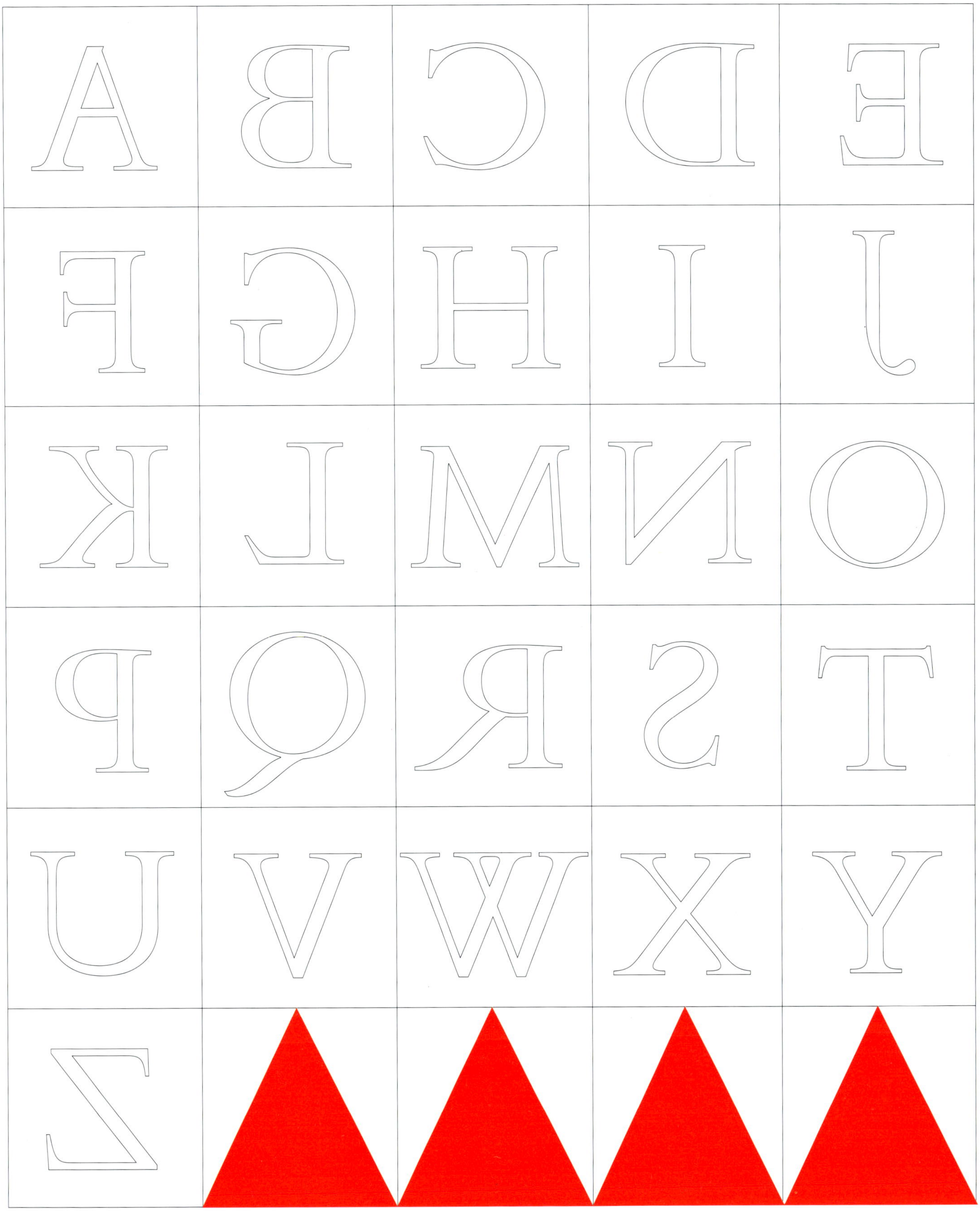

mobile

Apparently newborn babies respond to black and white before colour and recognize faces before any other shape. This mobile combines the two. So many mobiles are designed to be viewed straight on, but look like nothing more than a bunch of twirling blobs from underneath. This one is meant to be hung above the bassinet, and offers its best view to the baby below. The gently circling faces with their range of expressions are enchanting and quite mesmerising.

materials

- 6 wooden disks about 10cm (4in) in diameter and 3mm (1/8in) thick (available from craft suppliers)

NOTE ✿ if you have a jigsaw or scrollsaw, you could cut out your own disks

- Acrylic paint in black and white
- Paint brushes 10mm (size 12), 3mm (size 5) and 1mm (size 000)
- Six 5mm (3/16in) screw eyes
- Bamboo or wire ring 25cm (10in) in diameter
- Fishing line
- Varnish

preparation

Sand the wooden disks if necessary.

Paint a white base coat. If required, repeat with a second coat when dry. Trace faces onto disks, or draw your own, and paint in the features in black.

TIP ✿ If you are not confident with a paintbrush, you could use a black marker pen for the details. An easy way out is to photocopy these patterns and simply cut them out, glue them onto the wooden disks and varnish.

Allow disks to dry before brushing them with one or more coats of clear varnish.

Turn the disks face down and put a screw eye into the exact centre of each. Paint the backs with a coat of black acrylic paint.

assembly

Mark four points at equal intervals around the bamboo or wire ring.

Cut a length of fishing line and tie one end securely to a point on the ring. Take the line across to the opposite point and attach firmly there. Tie a cross piece between the other two points in the same way. This gives you a centre point from which to attach another length of fishing line to hang your mobile.

Now mark six points at equal intervals around the ring. Attach fishing line very carefully to the screw eye on the back of each wooden disk. Tie each line to the ring, varying the length so that the faces hang at different levels. Make the shortest line about 18cm (7in) from the top, and the longest about 36cm (14in).

Suspend this mobile from the point where the crossed lines meet within the ring. It should hang flat but a slight tweaking may be necessary.

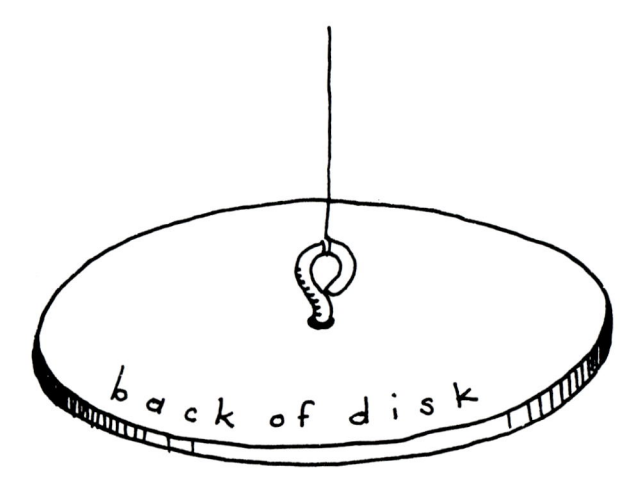

back of disk

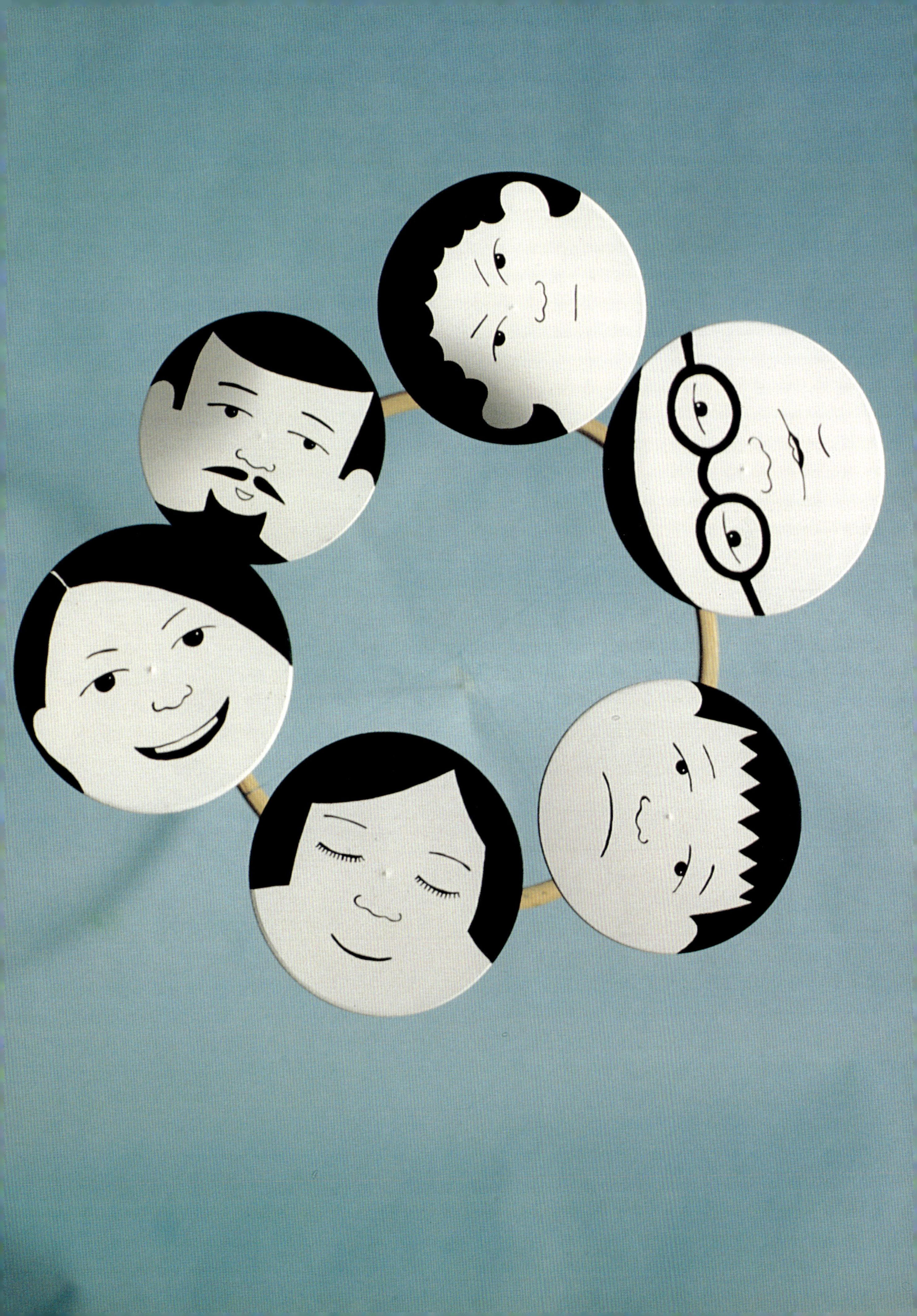

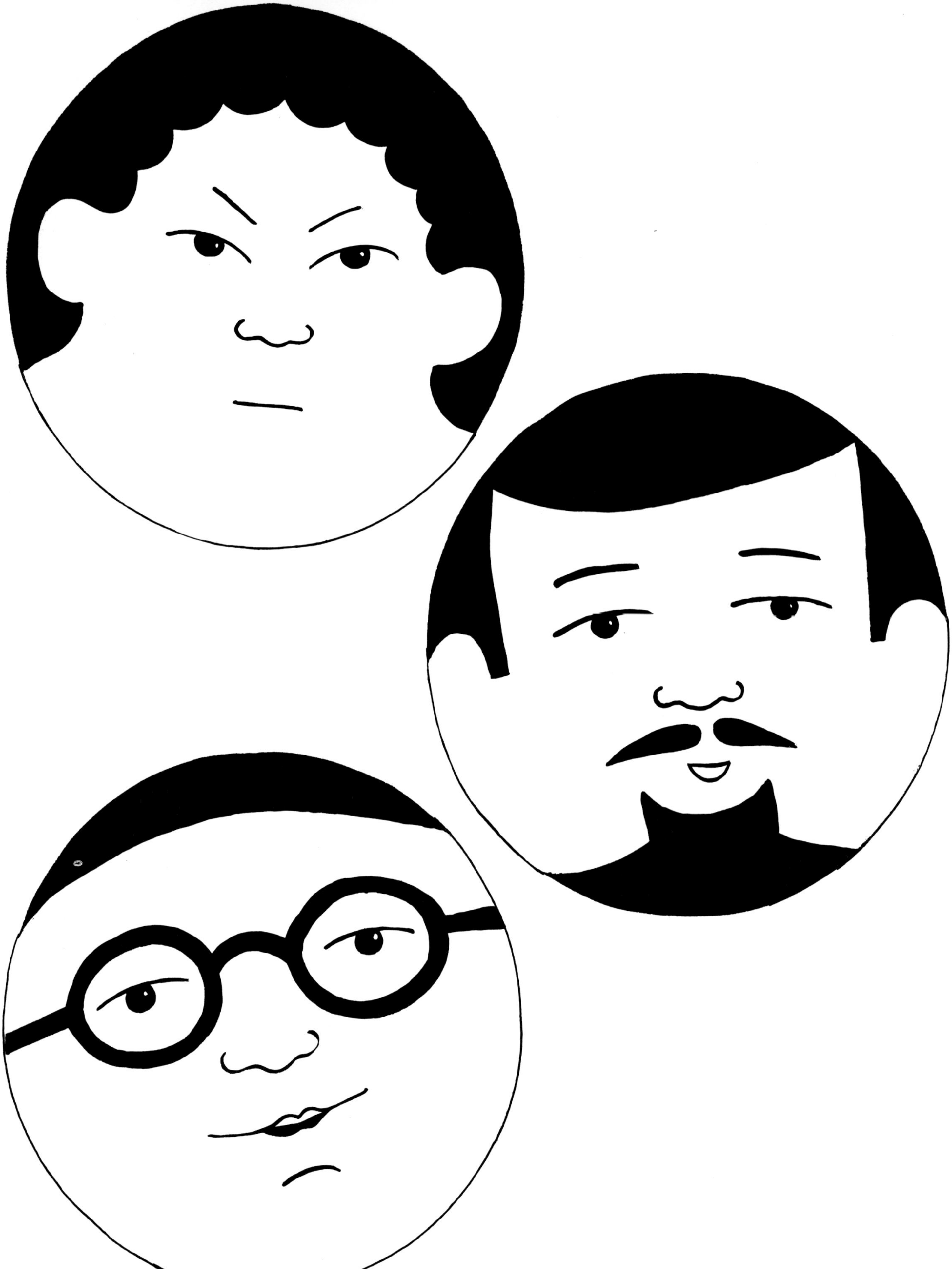

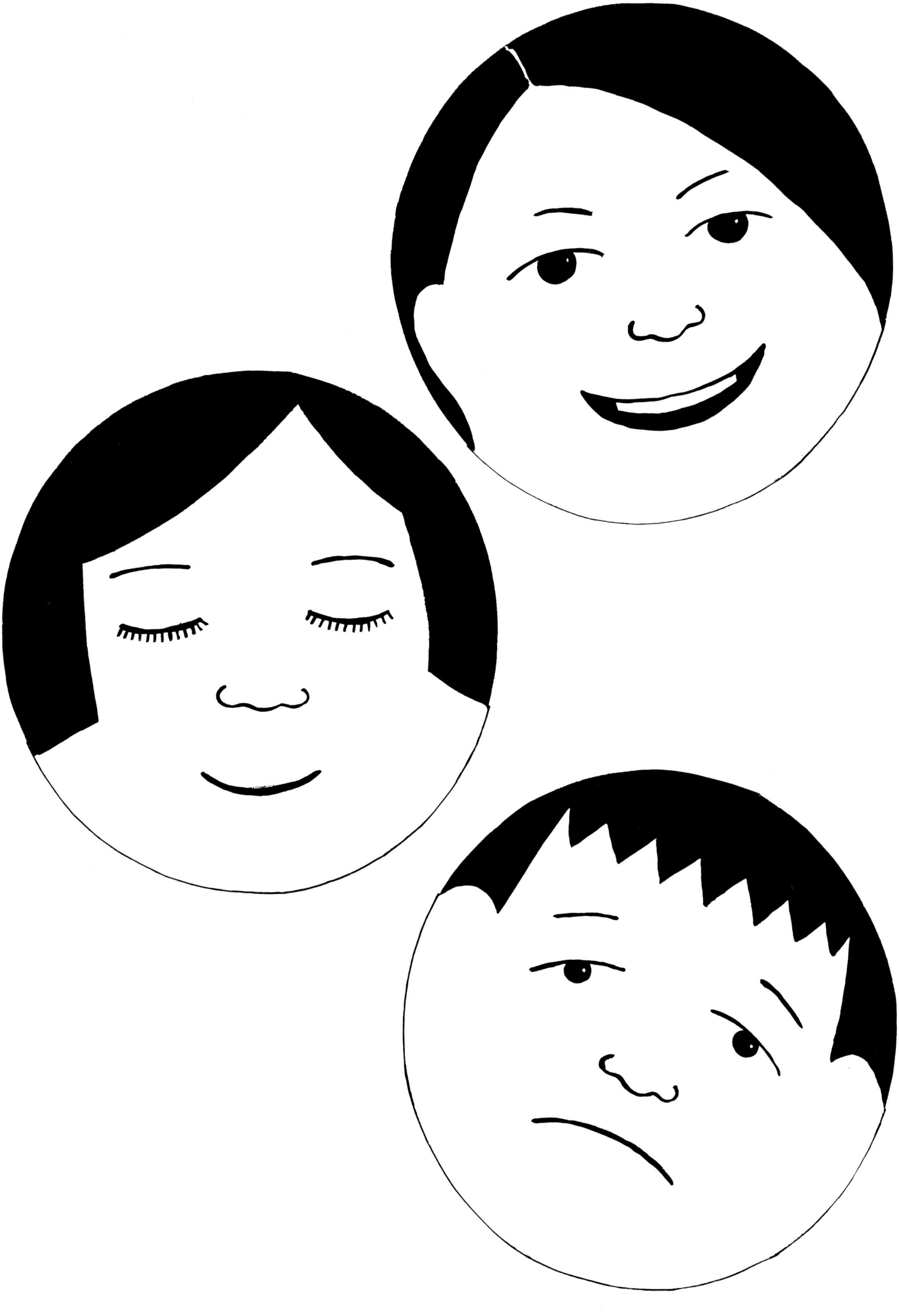

dragonfly
caterpillar
worm
lady bird
bee
bug
butterfly
tiny lizard
grasshopper
beetle
ant
moth
snail
little friends
frog

insect quilt

This quilt need not be made in a hurry, but is a lovely thing to pick up when the armchair calls and you feel like a bit of cosy hand sewing. I recommend beginning with one or two of the appliquéd insects before you rush to measure out linen and batting. (If you find them in a cupboard in a few years' time, they can always be turned into cushions; I have several cushions that never matured into quilts). It is very satisfying to watch the quilt take shape as you complete each insect, and at that stage it only takes a bit of machine sewing to assemble the finished product.

materials

- 100cm x 175cm (40in x 70in) linen
- 100cm x 175cm (40in x 70in) backing fabric (in a small red check)
- 100cm x 175cm (40in x 70in) polyester or wool batting (if you do not have a preference, ask your supplier for guidance)
- 175cm (70in) red cotton
- 150cm (60in) white cotton drill
- Approximately 20cm (8in) cotton fabric in each of the following colours: yellow, orange, bright red, dark red, pink, light turquoise, dark turquoise, dark green, light green, pale green, pale blue, light blue, dark blue, bright blue, khaki, beige, grey, black and brown
- Sewing thread in a range of colours
- Black and red embroidery thread
- Quilting pins (long pins with round heads)

preparation

Before you begin, wash and iron all fabrics keeping coloureds, white and linen separate. The best way to tackle this quilt is insect by insect, completing each block before you move onto the next.

You will notice that each piece of the pattern is numbered and coloured. The numbers refer to the order in which you place the pieces on the background block (more on that later) and the colours speak for themselves.

Begin by dissecting the pattern into colours and assembling fabrics. Trace each element of the insect pattern (following dotted lines as necessary) onto paper and cut out. Pin each pattern to its respective colour of fabric and cut out, 5mm (¼in) from edge.

Measure a rectangular block of the appropriate dimensions for each insect (see table on page 85) and cut out of white cotton drill adding 1.5cm (⅝in) all around. Fold the block in half twice (horizontally then vertically) and press lightly to determine your positioning guidelines.

Arrange coloured fabric pieces on this white background in numerical order, putting the first down then overlapping subsequent pieces as shown in the pattern. For example, the bee's body is made from a basic black shape, with yellow stripes appliquéd over the top. Play around with the pieces until you are satisfied with the arrangement, remembering that you will lose about 5mm (¼in) off each piece when you stitch them down. Pin each piece in place.

To appliqué the insect blocks...

As most of these insect designs have sharp corners and tight curves, the easiest way to hand sew them is to use a method called needle-turned appliqué. This involves using the point of the needle to turn the raw edges under as they are stitched down to the background fabric.

First clip into corners and curves with sharp scissors. Begin with the uppermost piece. Using the point of the needle, turn under the raw edge of the fabric piece just ahead of stitching and flatten with your thumb. Catch the folded edge down. Continue to appliqué each piece in this manner.

Embroider eyes with French knots (see page 37 for instructions) and mouths in a straight stitch. Embroider the name of the insect with black thread, also in a straight stitch.

Make up each insect block in this way.

Press the edges of each block under by 1.5cm (⅝in).

assembly

To assemble the quilt...

If you haven't already done so, cut the linen, the backing fabric and the batting to size.

Spread the linen for the front of the quilt out on your bed or the floor, or any flat, clean surface.

Arrange the blocks on the linen (refer to photograph for positional guide) pin down and tack.

Use the red embroidery thread to work decorative blanket stitch around the blocks, simultaneously attaching them to the linen.

Remove tacking. Clip any threads that remain, and give the whole piece a final press.

Sandwich batting between the linen and the backing fabric (right sides outwards) and make sure all layers are smooth.

Starting in the middle, pin all three layers together -this is where the long quilter's pins are especially useful. Work radiating out towards the edges, inserting pins at regular intervals (about every 7cm [2¾in]) smoothing out wrinkles and working excess fullness to the outside. Turn over periodically to check that backing is as smooth as the front of the quilt.

To quilt...

With pins in place, baste around the perimeter of each block and in between the rows.

Machine quilt (or hand quilt if you have the time or inclination) around each block, just outside the blanket stitch. This is actually quite easy and very quick and providing you have secured all three layers together thoroughly, the fabric shouldn't shift about. This is the basic amount of quilting which will hold the layers together and keep the batting evenly distributed. If you develop a taste for it, you could continue with a second row of stitching around each block or introduce some decorative edges.

To make the binding...

To determine the amount of binding you will need, measure the perimeter of your quilt and add 40cm (16in) for mitred corners and finished ends (approximately 550cm [6yd]).

As this quilt has straight sides and is made with mitred corners, the binding will be straight-grain, which is easier to make than bias binding.

Rule and cut 10cm (4in) wide strips either from across the fabric (widthwise) or down the length the fabric (lengthwise).

TIP ✿ Strips cut across the width are easier to work with as they have more give, however, cutting on the lengthwise grain gives you longer strips which means fewer joins.

To join strips, place two ends perpendicular to each other with right sides together. Sew across the strips (see diagram), to make a diagonal seam. Trim 6mm (¼in) from stitch line and press seam open. Continue until you have one continuous strip.

Press the strip of binding in half lengthwise with the wrong sides together.

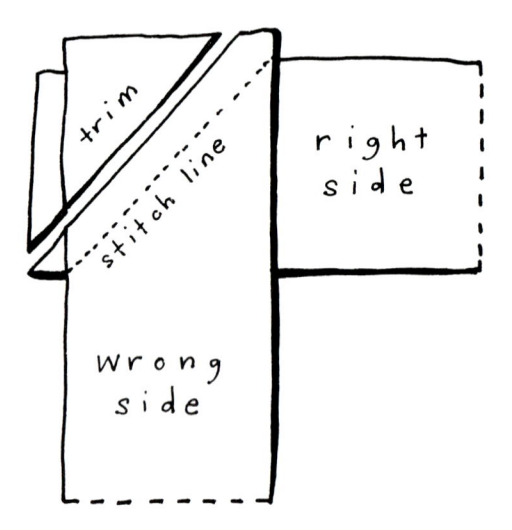

To bind the edges of the quilt...

TIP ✿ If your sewing machine has a walking foot attachment, this is an ideal time to use it. The walking foot keeps layers of fabric from slipping.

If you don't have the walking foot attachment, hand baste the edges of the quilt together, or pin carefully at regular intervals, either of which will prevent the layers from shifting.

Start somewhere along one side of the quilt rather than at a corner as this is difficult to finish neatly. Align the binding to the quilt, with right sides and raw edges together. The folded edge will be to the left of the sewing line.

Begin sewing about 12cm (4¾in) from the beginning point, leaving this first section loose for joining later. Sew 2cm (¾in) in from the edge.

To mitre the corners…

When you approach a corner, stop sewing 2cm (¾in) in from the edge and backstitch.

TIP ❁ Put pins in corners 2cm (¾in) from each edge to use as a guide.

Remove quilt from the sewing machine and rotate 90°. Fold binding straight up from the corner (see diagram) forming a 45° angle fold. Bring binding down over this fold, in line with the next edge to be sewn. The top fold should be even with the raw edge of the side you were sewing last.

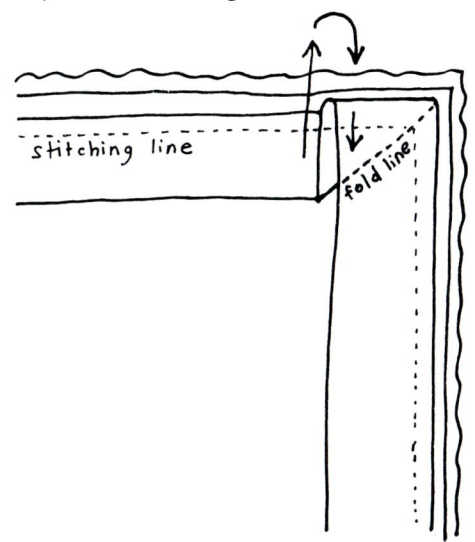

Begin sewing again at the top of this edge 2cm (¾in) in as before. Repeat for the other three corners.

To finish binding…

When you return to your starting point, join the binding ends together with a folding edge. To do this, fold the excess you left at the beginning back on itself. Lay the end of the binding over this fold and continue sewing about 3cm (1¼in) beyond it. Trim excess from both ends to 6mm (¼in) from the seam.

To hand finish quilt…

If necessary, trim the edges to make them even. Fold the binding over the edge to the back of the quilt, so that it just covers the machine stitching, and catch it down by hand with discreet stitches.

When you reach the corner, fold the binding from the next side under to form a 45° angle (and a mitred corner). Continue to the end. Stitch down all mitred corners on front and back.

If you want to, embroider your baby's name and date of birth at the bottom of the quilt.

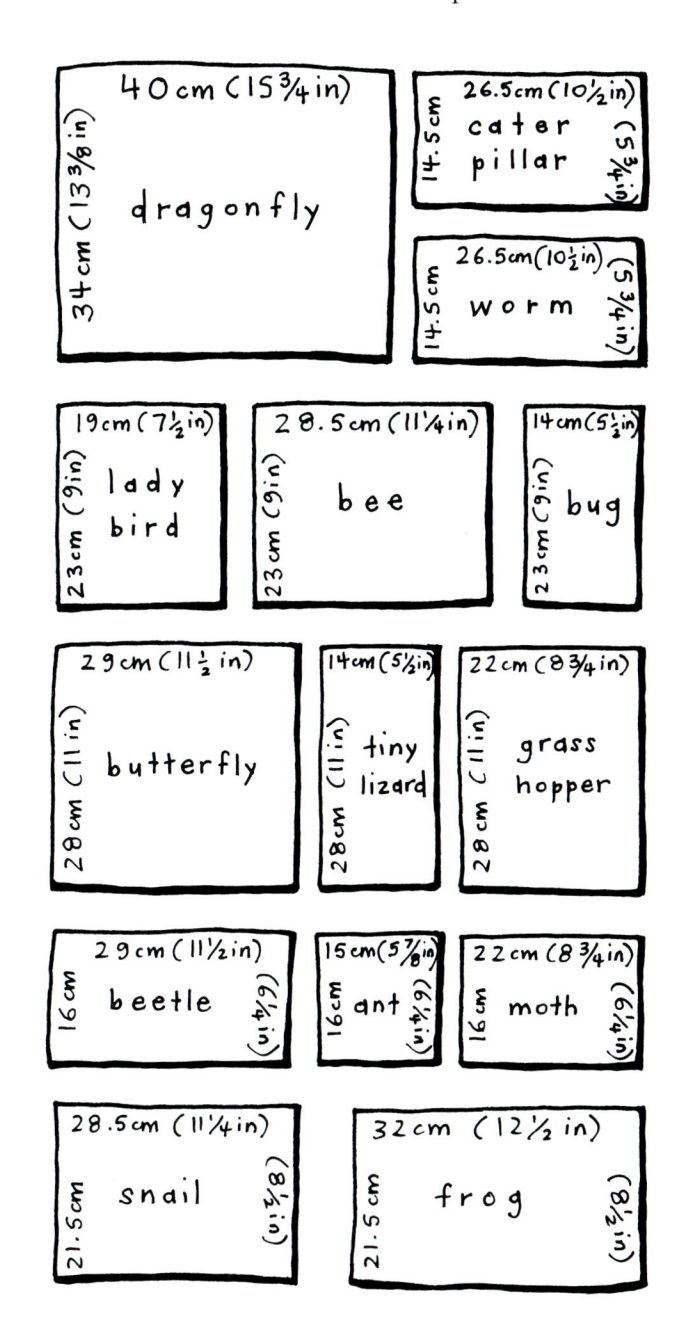

Block	Width	Height
dragonfly	40cm (15¾in)	34cm (13⅜in)
caterpillar	26.5cm (10½in)	14.5cm (5¾in)
worm	26.5cm (10½in)	14.5cm (5¾in)
ladybird	19cm (7½in)	23cm (9in)
bee	28.5cm (11¼in)	23cm (9in)
bug	14cm (5½in)	23cm (9in)
butterfly	29cm (11½in)	28cm (11in)
tiny lizard	14cm (5½in)	28cm (11in)
grasshopper	22cm (8¾in)	28cm (11in)
beetle	29cm (11½in)	16cm (6¼in)
ant	15cm (5⅞in)	16cm (6¼in)
moth	22cm (8¾in)	16cm (6¼in)
snail	28.5cm (11¼in)	21.5cm (8½in)
frog	32cm (12½in)	21.5cm (8½in)

bee
wing 10
wing 1
wing 2
wing 9
stripe 7
stripe 5
body 3
stripe 4
eye 14
head 8
stripe 6
leg 13
leg 11
leg 12

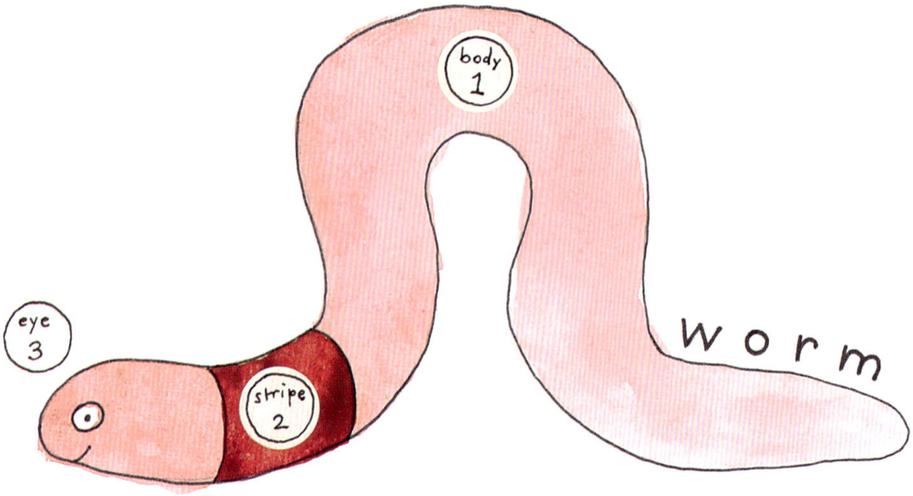
body 1
eye 3
worm
stripe 2

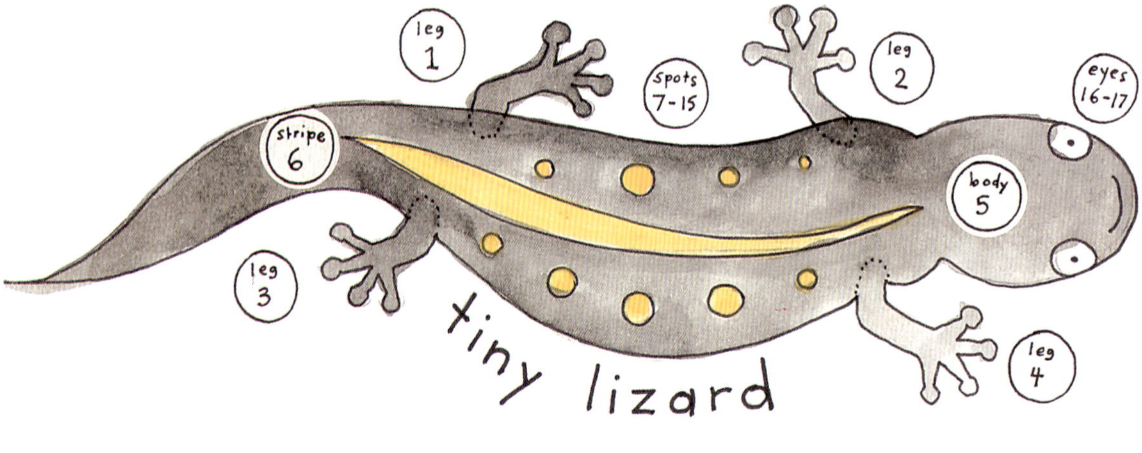
leg 1
leg 2
spots 7-15
eyes 16-17
stripe 6
body 5
leg 3
leg 4
tiny lizard

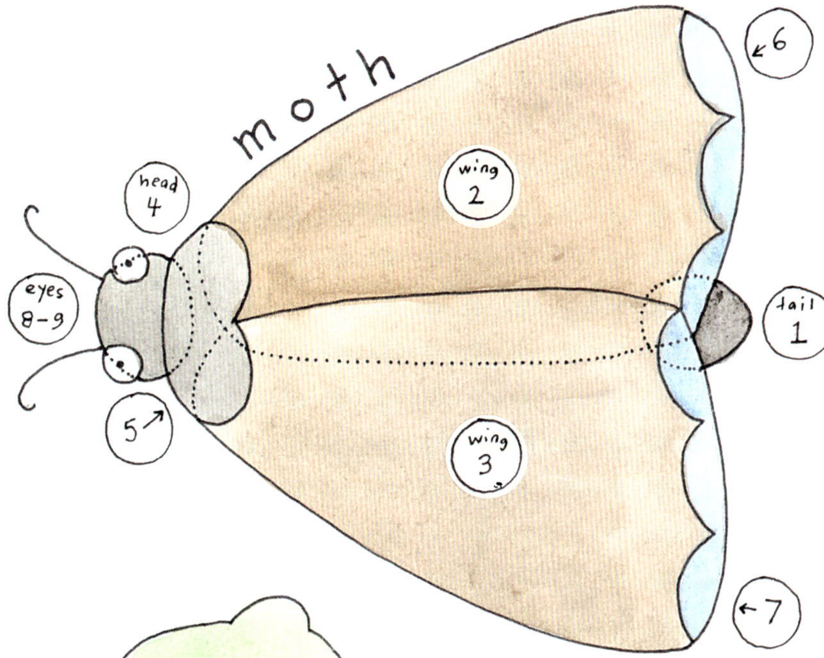
moth
head 4
eyes 8–9
5
wing 2
wing 3
6
tail 1
7

frog
spots 15–23
eye 24
3
front leg 4
stripes 5–7
1
2
stripes 9–14
back leg 8

grasshopper
back knee 1
back leg 7
head 6
wing 5
eye 10
body 4
leg 8
under leg 2
leg 9
back leg 3

butterfly
7
upper wing 3
spots 16-20
eyes 30-31
crescents 10-12
lower wing 1
body 9
5
l.wing 2
u.wing 4
big spots 26-27
little spots 28-29
6
8
crescents 13-15
spots 21-25
bug
body 1
grey 2
stripes 4-6
head 3
eyes 7-8
ant
eye 4
body 1
red 2
head 3
snail
5
4
3
6
body 2
eye 7
belly 1

dragonfly

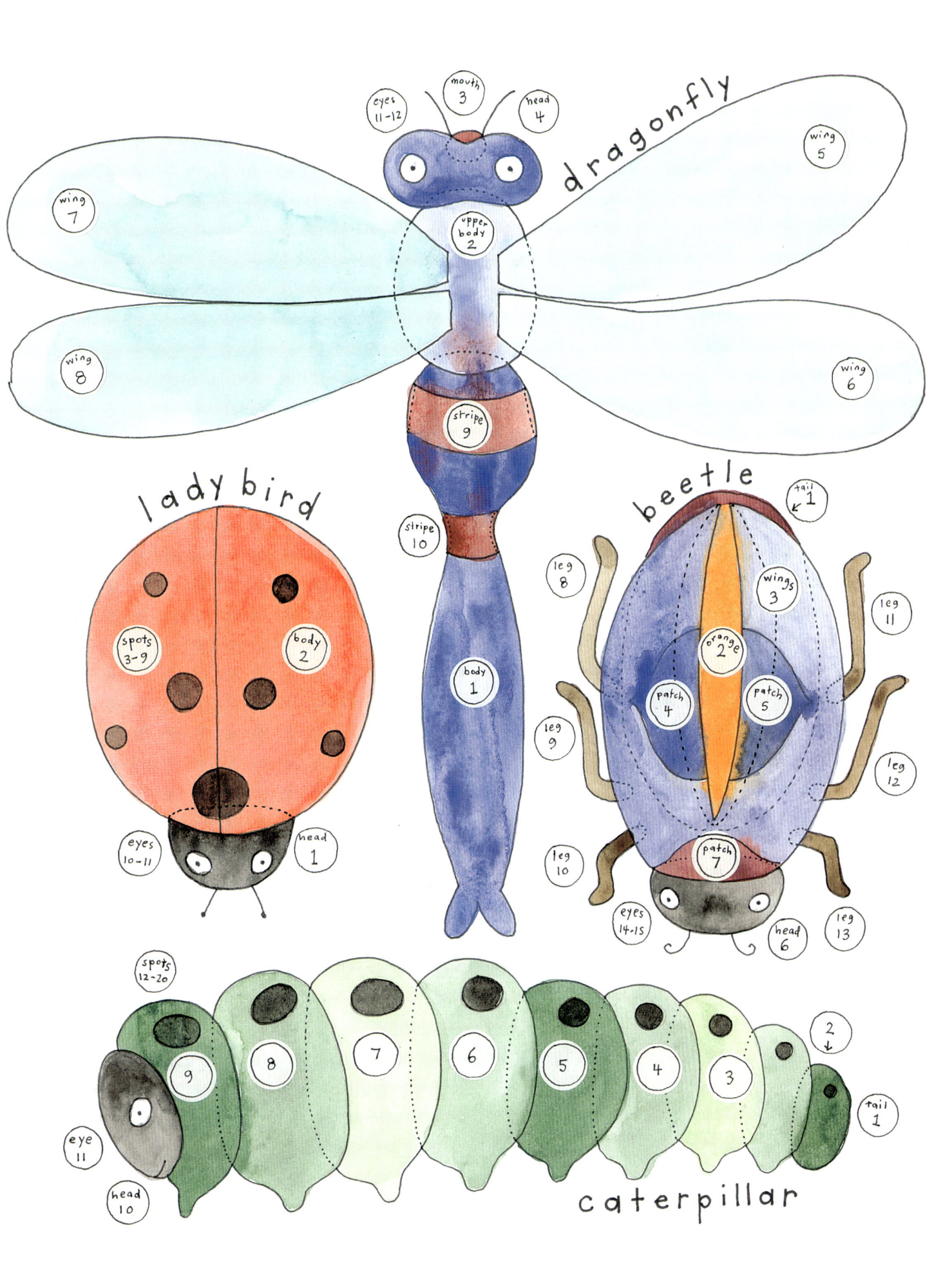

ladybird

beetle

caterpillar

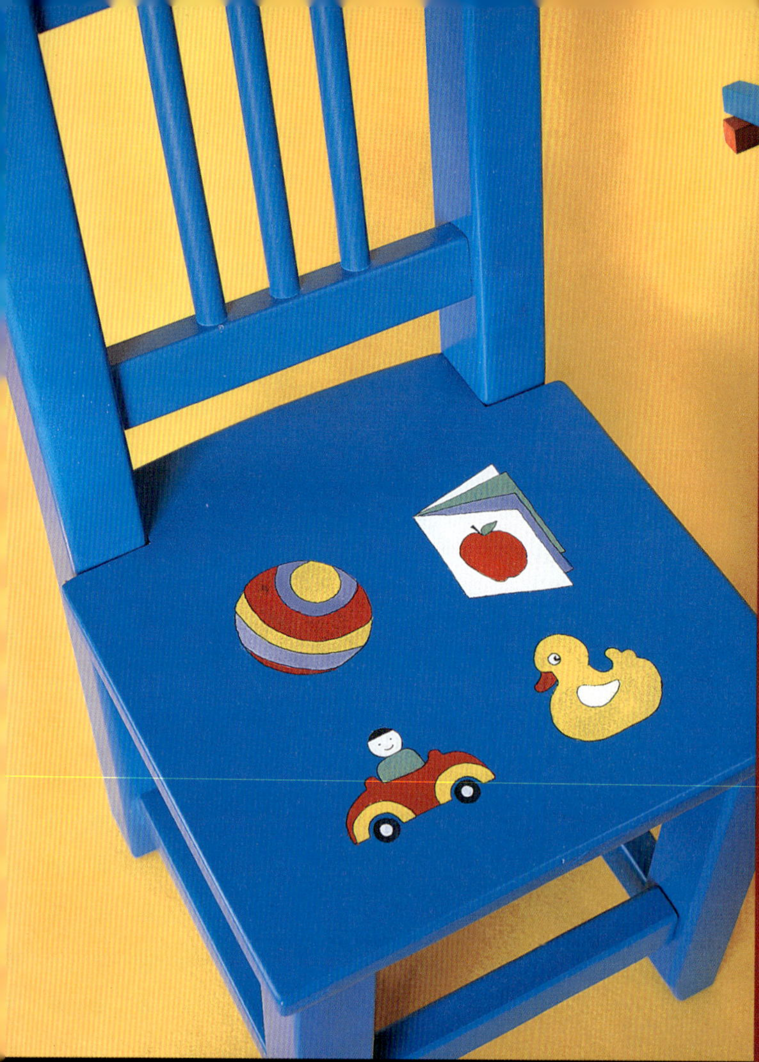
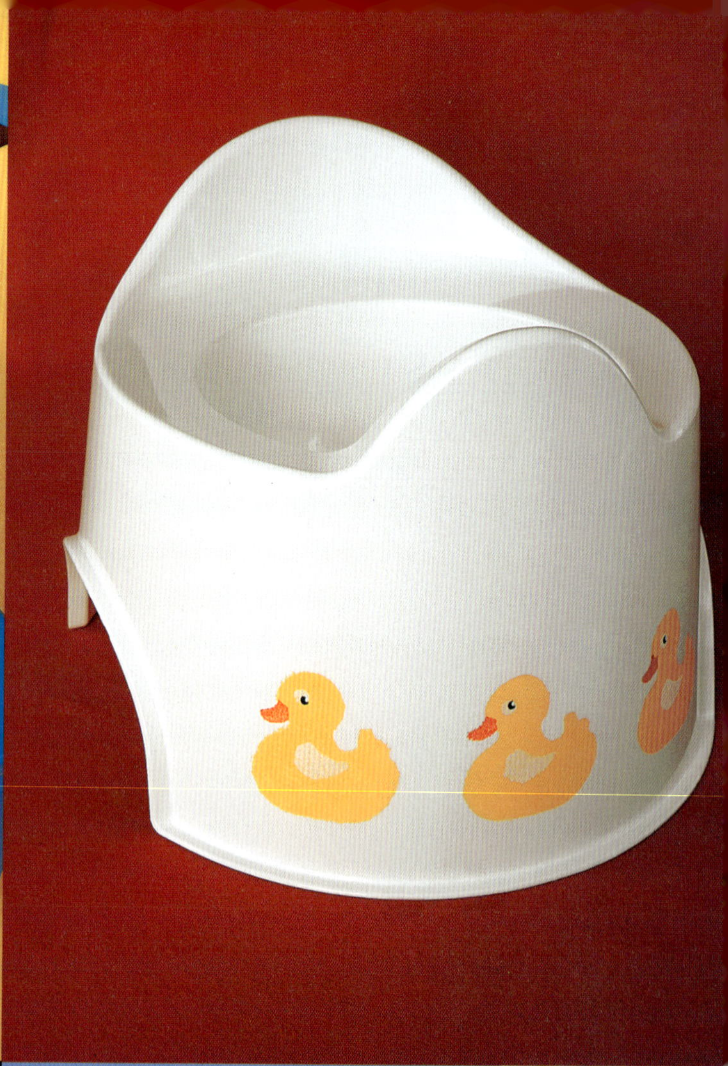
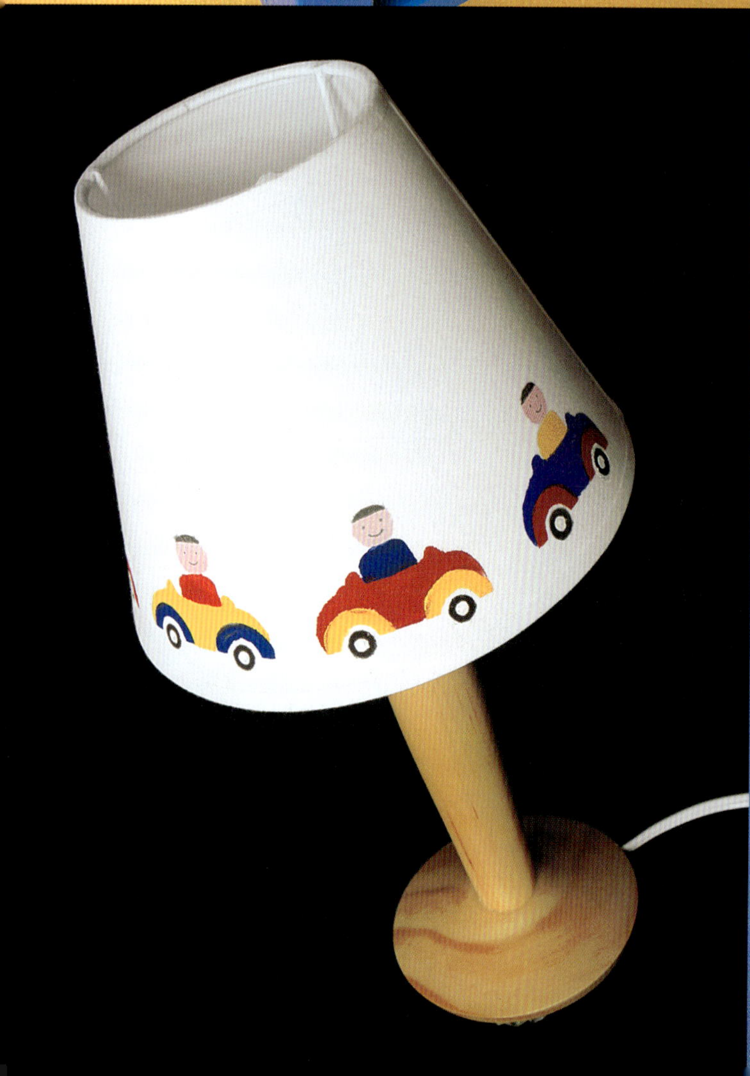
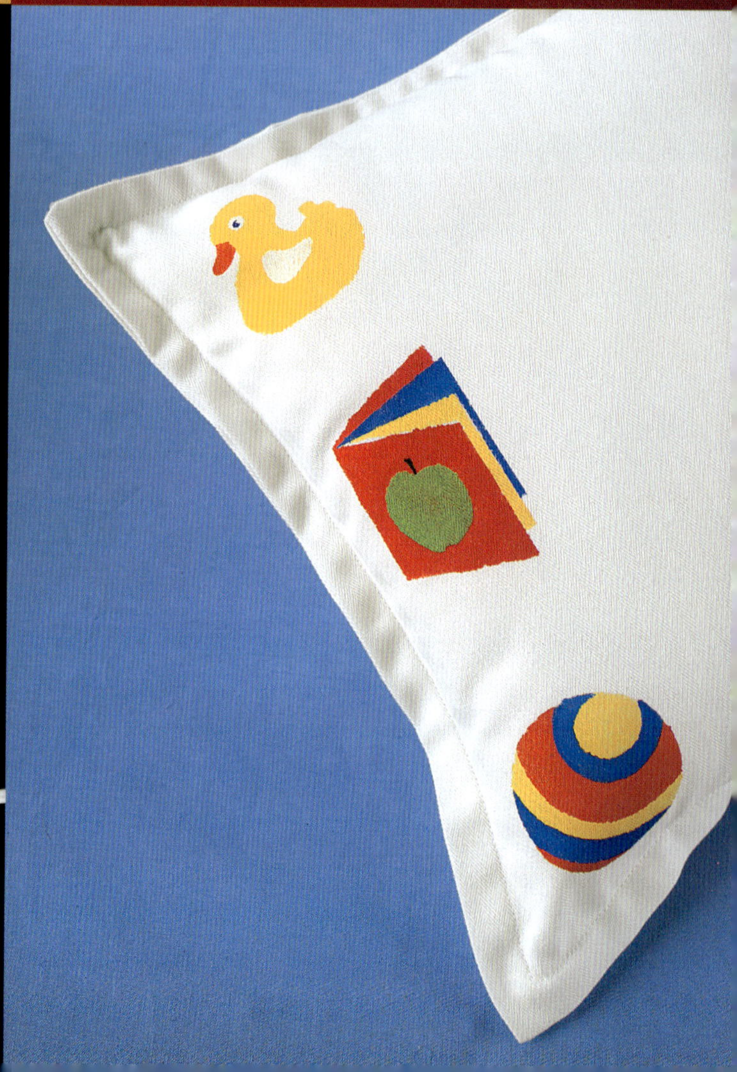

stencils

Stencilling is an easy and effective way of printing and repeating a design on almost any surface. As you gain confidence, you can progress from simple shapes in single colours to quite complex designs with many colours in layers. You can purchase specific stencilling materials from art and craft supply stores, but you can also make your own from inexpensive stationery and household items. Both options are described under materials. Many of the patterns in this book could be used as stencil designs, either just as they are, or with a few adjustments.

materials

There are four main elements to stencilling:
- The stencil itself
- The brush or sponge
- The paint
- The surface to be stencilled

stencils

Professional stencils are made from **acetate**, a transparent plastic available by the sheet from art suppliers, or from a **waxed cardboard** which resists moisture from paint. It is much easier to use acetate as you need only place the design underneath and trace using an overhead transparency marker or any pen that will write on plastic without smearing.

The waxed cardboard is less expensive but also less durable. Also, to transfer the design you need to use carbon paper between the pattern and the cardboard or draw freehand directly onto it.

Another alternative which is inexpensive and accessible, is the **clear adhesive plastic film** often used to cover schoolbooks. Simply cover the photocopied design on both sides with the film, smoothing out any bubbles or creases. The stencil is protected from moisture but is still flexible, which is useful when you are printing something three dimensional such as the lampshade opposite.

brushes and sponges

Proper **stencil brushes** have short firm bristles tightly packed together. You hold the brush upright and apply the paint with a dabbing motion.

For a more textured or varied finish the paint can be applied with a **sponge**, either an irregularly formed natural sea sponge or a more uniform manufactured sponge. I have achieved excellent results using a simple household **cleaning sponge** cut into squares.

paint

The type of paint you use will really depend on what you are stencilling. Flat acrylic paints are suitable for most surfaces such as wooden furniture or plaster walls. If the walls need to be washable, you should consider using an interior house paint. If the object to be stencilled is likely to receive a certain amount of wear and tear it is a very good idea to protect your work with a few coats of clear varnish.

To stencil onto fabric, you should either use special fabric paints or a medium to mix with your ordinary acrylics. Ask your art supplier for guidance.

the surface

Almost any surface can be stencilled! For something dramatic consider a frieze around the nursery walls or a design on the floor if you have floorboards. Smaller projects could be children's furniture, lampshades, sheets or pillows. You could stencil a repeat pattern onto plain fabric and make it up into cutains or baby clothes.

preparation

When you have transferred your design to the stencil, either by tracing the image onto acetate or by one of the other methods described, carefully cut out the segments of the design with a craft knife. Remember that the 'bridges' which separate the segments are the lines which give the image definition, so it is important to keep them intact.

When a design has two or more colours, each colour should have its own stencil. Trace appropriate segments and a few key lines from adjacent segments to use as a guide when positioning the stencil before applying the second colour. Label each piece of the stencil with the name of the colour to be used.

TIP ✿ When cutting stencils, use a board or mat to protect the surface beneath. Cut towards you, turning the stencil away from you as you work.

applying paint

Before you begin, prepare the surface to be stencilled. If it is a wooden object, sand if necessary. Make sure all fabric has been washed and ironed prior to being stencilled. All surfaces should be clean and dust free.

Position the stencil where you want the design to go and tape in place if necessary.

TIP ✿ It is a good idea to practise on paper before you begin to stencil. This allows you to see how the colours will look and to work out how much paint you need on the brush or sponge. You could keep the paper prints and use them for birthday cards.

The brush or sponge should be almost dry, and the paint dabbed on lightly. Whether you use a brush or a sponge, you will achieve better results by applying paint in thin layers. A heavy layer will tend to bleed around the edges of the stencil, smudging the design.

TIP ✿ Thin layers will also dry faster, allowing you to get on with applying the next colour.

After each application, wipe the stencil clean with a damp cloth or paper towel. This will make it last longer and also prevents areas getting clogged giving a neater, more professional result.

For multicoloured designs, stencil the large base areas first then build the foreground layers of colour. Try to choose lighter colours which can be overlaid with increasingly darker ones.

Allow each layer to dry before applying the next.

Don't forget to set all fabric paint according to the manufacturer's directions.

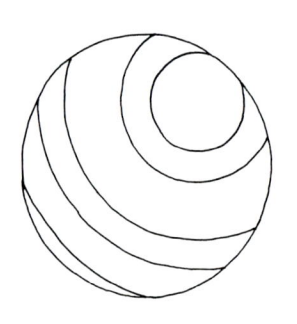